FIDGET!

101 Ways to Boost Your Creativity
and Decrease Your Stress

HEATHER FISHEL

ADAMS MEDIA

NEW YORK   LONDON   TORONTO   SYDNEY   NEW DELHI

Adams Media
An Imprint of Simon & Schuster, Inc.
57 Littlefield Street
Avon, Massachusetts 02322

First Adams Media trade paperback edition JANUARY 2018

ADAMS MEDIA and colophon are trademarks of Simon and Schuster.

For information about special discounts for bulk purchases, please contact Simon & Schuster Special Sales at 1-866-506-1949 or business@simonandschuster.com.

The Simon & Schuster Speakers Bureau can bring authors to your live event. For more information or to book an event contact the Simon & Schuster Speakers Bureau at 1-866-248-3049 or visit our website at www.simonspeakers.com.

Interior design by Colleen Cunningham
Interior illustrations by Nicola DosSantos

Manufactured in the United States of America

10 9 8 7 6 5 4 3 2 1

Library of Congress Cataloging-in-Publication Data
Fishel, Heather, author.
Fidget! / Heather Fishel.
Avon, Massachusetts: Adams Media, 2018.
LCCN 2017040183 | ISBN 9781507206010 (pb) | ISBN 9781507206027 (ebook)
LCSH: Distraction (Psychology) | Mental fatigue. | Stress management. | Creative ability.
LCC BF323.D5 F57 2018 | DDC 155.9/042--dc23
LC record available at https://lccn.loc.gov/2017040183

ISBN 978-1-5072-0601-0
ISBN 978-1-5072-0602-7 (ebook)

CONTENTS

INTRODUCTION

Ever catch yourself fidgeting? Do you gnaw at the tip of your pen while you work? Are you prone to staring out the nearest window, more immersed in the sights and sounds outside than the computer screen in front of you? Have you been guilty of bouncing in your chair to the beat of your favorite song while tackling tasks? Two pieces of good news: you're not alone, and you've picked up the right book!

Nearly everyone becomes distracted when they try to maintain concentration for a long period of time. Behavioral scientists tell us that many of today's jobs, schools, and lifestyles put us in unnatural positions—literally: neither our brains nor our bodies were made to focus for countless hours on end. We were made to move around. The long periods of sitting, the lack of changes in our physical and mental scenery—they're enough to test anyone's attention reserves.

Commanding yourself to "Just focus!" isn't enough to boost your concentration on your work: we all know this because we've tried it untold times. Often, the solution to wandering thoughts or a fading attention span isn't found in orders or instructions to ourselves, or even in words at all. We can feel it in our bodies—they want to move!

Where we once fought those urges to move, doodle, stare, and daydream, more and more of us are realizing that the only way out is to give in to our fidgety urges. Research increasingly confirms it: let your body move, your brain daydream, your hand doodle, and you'll become more productive, more creative, and more engaged over the long haul.

Fidgeting is the body's way of dealing with the sedentary habits that have become increasingly common in twenty-first-century life. For the most part, we have trained ourselves to sit and concentrate when we perform any kind of task—to address the challenge by pressing the focus button until we're done. You may even agree that a key sign of a great work ethic is a person's ability to labor over a task without any sign of distraction until the work is done. This approach may look appealing, but it's not very efficient or effective: neuroscience tells us that the more repetitive and boring a task is, the more likely your brain is to tune out. When we sit stationary in front of a computer screen for hours on end or stuff hundreds of envelopes in one sitting, we're practically begging our minds to start wandering. When they wander off on their own and focus is completely lost, experts estimate that it can take as long as 25 minutes for us to return our full attention to a task, wasting precious time and exhausting our limited resources.

We should be fidgeting instead! Long misunderstood as a telltale sign of an undisciplined mind, fidgeting is enjoying a complete rethinking by cognitive and behavioral researchers, educators, and maybe even a parent or two. In this book, you'll come across familiar fidgets, some others you've never thought of, and maybe even a few you've been doing all your life without realizing it! In reading through them, you'll understand a bit better just what you're getting out of that doodling or pacing and discover some new ways to fidget that just might be perfect for you.

So what counts as fidgeting? According to Purdue University, fidgeting is what we're up to when we do two things simultaneously: one activity focuses part of the brain on the most important action, while the second utilizes an entirely different part of the brain and body to dispense with static, or built-up, frustrated energy. That second activity—the fidget—frees up the main part of the brain to devote its focus to the important project at hand. Even though it seems counterintuitive, distraction and loss of focus often arise not because we're out of energy, but because we've got too much mental and physical energy that isn't used up in the process of doing whatever it is we're focused on. When our feet start tapping or our eyes begin to roam around, our bodies are telling us they need somewhere to release all that excess energy. They need to fidget.

In fact, allowing yourself to fidget in any way—doodling across a notepad, rubbing a smooth stone, kicking the legs of your chair—promotes more creative thought, speedier learning, and improved focus. Studies have also found that fidgeting enhances concentration, relieves stress and anxiety, and inspires creative thinking. The key may be finding the fidget that works best for you. Different fidgets connect with different parts of our brains and bodies, solving different problems and demonstrating different benefits. Repetitive fidgets, like toe tapping, can be calming, while playing with something that clicks can jolt your attention back to a task. As long as the movement, activity, scene, or sound doesn't distract you or require your full attention, just about any fidget will help boost your productivity and expand your potential.

So grab this book, tap your feet, and get ready to fidget!

PART 1

MOVEMENT

BOUNCING, TAPPING, DOODLING, AND OTHER PHYSICAL FIDGETS

Squirming, tapping, clicking, pen chewing: these behaviors are the bane of teachers, parents, and managers worldwide. Chances are, if you're someone who needs to fidget, you've been yelled at a few times to put down your pen and stop scribbling. You may have received a side-eye or two as you drummed your fingers on your desk during a meeting or scrawled images of trees, cats, or underwater landscapes instead of actually taking notes. Though "frivolous" physical movement is typically misperceived as a sign of inattentiveness, it often signals just the opposite: the fidgeter's desperate attempt to stay on track.

Movements like bouncing, tapping, and writing come with a whole host of mental benefits, including improved concentration, increased productivity for employees, and enhanced creative thought. Movement fidgeting is even thought to boost listening skills—and it's fun.

Psychologist Abigail Levrini explains that movement helps release excess energy and offers relief to the brain. The more we attempt to focus without moving or giving in to distraction, the faster our minds become exhausted. Allow yourself to wiggle, bounce, or walk, and you'll feel less mental stress. Further research indicates that doodling frees up both short- and long-term memory—improving information retention—and that even the tiniest of movements spark the release of dopamine and norepinephrine, neurochemicals known to sharpen focus. And though it might give the appearance that you're ready to give up, moving around while working isn't evidence of distraction. Rather, fidgeting with your hands or feet turns part of your attention away from a concept that's taxing you and lets different parts of your brain come to understand these challenging new ideas with the aid of distraction. Movement fidgeting, in essence, helps you tune out exhausting details and simultaneously zero in on the bigger picture.

Physical fidgeting is often spontaneous, and it should be. However, there are situations in which actively choosing to fidget is smarter than forcing yourself to sit still. Go ahead and fidget—quietly, of course—during lessons, presentations, meetings, and even phone calls. Any time you're listening to someone speak and find your focus beginning to wane, it's a smart idea to get a part of your body moving. Just make certain you aren't drawing all the attention in the room to the bouncing of your feet or the whirring of your fidget spinner! The next time your coworker or your boss cracks a joke about your doodle-filled notes or wonders why you need to walk to the watercooler every half hour, don't let it bother you. Physical fidgeting is firing up your brain, improving your memory, and inspiring you to be your most creative.

DOODLE WEIRD AND RANDOM NEW CREATIONS

Has a coworker ever looked over at your notepad and smirked at your scrawls of fish swimming through kelp or your dolphins splashing out of ocean waves? Have teachers taken offense at your assignments featuring surprise drawings of your favorite flowers and blooming greenery? Random doodles, though often a little out of place in a professional or traditional academic setting, serve a great purpose: they can introduce new ideas, perspectives, and angles. As you doodle, practice mixing and matching unrelated concepts and thoughts to create funny, strange, and entirely new inventions. Feel free to get weird with your doodles—they don't need to be related to the topic at hand. This can be a tricky one to get the hang of, but keep at it. For example, you could:

- Put a flamingo's stick-thin legs on an elephant
- Scribble a pair of cat ears on a leafy tree
- Add a unicorn horn to a sketch of yourself
- Draw an underwater scene set in a forest, not an ocean
- Transplant your blooming flower garden onto the moon

These odd mash-ups will encourage your brain to think in unique ways. As a result, you'll start seeing beyond the typical and conventional. Weird and wacky doodles are especially helpful when listening to dull information, like a droning lecture with no visual component. Your scribbled creations provide an outlet for your boredom, inspiring your brain to think in different ways while your ears continue to take in the information being discussed. ■

PACE WHILE YOU CHAT

The next time your phone rings, get up out of your chair and start walking. You can pace a set path or forge a new trail every time you take a call—either way, try to keep your feet moving for the duration of the conversation, whether it's out the door and around the block or just within the confines of your cubicle.

Walking while speaking and listening improves creative thinking, according to a Stanford University study, and gets ideas flowing more freely. The study results illustrated that participants who walked while talking experienced higher and more consistent levels of creativity compared to those who stayed seated.

So, whenever you answer a call or invite someone in for a brainstorming session, get up and go. Take a stroll around the café, wander on foot around your house, or circle the parking lot. You don't need to walk far—even pacing in a small circle around your cubicle at work boosts creative thought just as much as a lengthier walk. If possible, take your pacing outside for even more inspiration and creativity. While the physical movement of walking while talking should be the primary goal, stepping into a different environment is thought to offer a breath of cognitive fresh air. There's another bonus to pacing, too: by getting your body moving, you're adding steps and a little bit of exercise to your day! ∎

DRAW WHAT YOU HEAR

As you listen to a lecture or sit through a meeting, draw images of exactly what you're hearing. Really try to free your mind as you do this—whatever words seem "loudest" to your ear, those are the ones you should sketch, whether it's a crucial, central concept or a small piece of the larger message. This style of doodling helps you focus on the important pieces of complex ideas:

- Did someone mention a project's outcome with a significant cash increase? Draw dollar signs or stacks of bills.
- Are you learning something new in a training session, such as a new company policy on travel? Draw out the details, like an image of a credit card or a plane.
- Is your mind wandering while listening to the renovation plans for a new business? Sketch out a storefront, a table, and a chair or two as these details are mentioned.
- Trying to wrap your mind around the content of a literary lecture? Doodle important thematic points or keywords that describe what you need to know—shadows and sunlight to represent light and darkness, a frowny face for an evil character, or images that define a character, like a straw hat and a pair of overalls.

Unlike taking verbatim notes in words and letters, doodling specific images encourages the brain to see concepts in a different light. This doodle-fidget works for any listening setting, from watching a TED Talk online to chatting about party planning over brunch. ∎

GET SWIVELING IN YOUR OFFICE CHAIR

Most office or computer chairs have a built-in fidget feature: they swivel, allowing you to swing from side to side, if not completely around. While composing an email, working your way through a spreadsheet, or tackling a longer project, take advantage of the chair you're sitting in. Keep your hands focused on the keyboard as you swivel your seat, twisting right and left with the lower half of your body. You can also use the chair's wheels to move back and forth and laterally as you swivel.

The supposedly "silly" act of spinning in your seat can get you pumped to power through a tough workday.

Researchers think swiveling or rolling around in a moveable chair increases motivation to work, improves engagement, and boosts creativity. Swivel chairs have been added to classrooms throughout the US thanks to new studies that correlate student engagement and success with the ability to move, turn, and twist in their seats. Universities that provide swivel chairs in the classroom see students' motivation rise—and their grades increase too.

If you're stuck with a stationary chair, don't fret—you can still fidget for better focus. Turn your four-legged chair into something a little less ho-hum by cutting two tennis balls to fit onto the front or back legs. This will create a chair that wiggles just enough so you can lean from side to side and play with your balance, generating the same motivation, learning, and attention span benefits as a swivel chair. ∎

"ATOMIZE" CONCEPTS THROUGH DOODLES

Struggling to understand big ideas in a long-winded meeting or the romantic plot twists in a phone conversation with a friend? Scribble out your confusion with doodles! Turn your notepad into a fidget- and doodle-friendly center of understanding: take the concept at hand and break it down into its tiniest parts—its atoms, if you like.

For example, if you're trying to solve workplace woes in the messy break area, sketch out a piece of trash, a banana peel, or a dirty dish. Need to figure out how to fit twelve people at a table for eight? Draw each chair, each plate, each item that needs to fit on the tabletop. Trying to perfect your homemade ice cream? Break it down into doodles of milk, melted drops of liquid, and a cone.

These smaller elements generate new perspectives on items or ideas both familiar and perplexing. Atomized—or simplified—doodles guide the brain to temporarily stop considering the big picture in order to better understand the individual parts of a problem.

For example, breaking down big ideas can introduce new thoughts such as:

- Zeroing in on those pieces of trash and recognizing that assigning a dedicated person to empty the break room trash will prevent messy buildups.
- Examining the pieces involved in seating twelve people and discovering that you could introduce side tables to make more room.
- Removing an ingredient in a troublesome dish rather than finding the right one to balance it with.
- Seeing actual atoms drawn out to understand the individual building blocks comprising plants or objects. ■

MAP IT OUT

Overwhelmed with information or just bored out of your mind with numbers and data that aren't adding up? Doodle a map. You don't need to break out your geography or cartography skills—this fidget is about creating a process map (a visual display that illustrates a concept or a plan). Draw something in the vein of a Venn diagram or a flowchart and be sure to get creative.

Draw out the steps of your proposal as though they are small pieces that will go into the project you're building. Instead of using a traditional numbered or bullet-pointed list to organize your mental data, stick facts and details inside large arrows that lead to the big picture, or adopt a system of interlocking circles to highlight connections between different concepts.

Seeing pictures of a verbalized process or plan helps the brain make sense of complex systems and situations, sometimes much better than a bunch of words can. Viewing a map or outline in picture form also allows you to better remember the individual steps. Often, when trying to think of solutions for tricky problems, we end up hitting mental blocks that result in circling back through the same old ideas with little progress. Doodling a visual display, or road map, that shows the flow of events and individual pieces involved in a process helps bring the situation to life. ■

WRITE IT OUT WITH WORDS

Although doodling is often preferable to taking notes—which can be boring and even counterproductive for those who struggle to focus—the act of writing itself can be a form of fidgeting. After all, you're moving your hand while concentrating on a larger task. Writing words out while listening improves the brain's processing ability, and the motion also helps retain more information. Instead of following a traditional note-taking method that may not work for you, you can turn the process into a fidget that's exciting and mentally stimulating.

When you're sitting in a meeting, lecture, or conversation that requires your unwavering attention, fidget your way through with word "doodles" like these:

- Write down important words or phrases, not complete sentences.
- Turn big ideas into simpler concepts by summarizing them in no more than three to four words.
- Use your own words, not those of the person speaking—if the speaker uses words you would never use yourself, translate it into your own lingo.

Sticking to these steps provides the fidget-able foundation you need to absorb dull content. People who are selective in the words that they write down during meetings demonstrate better information recall down the road and tend to be more engaged with the material than their peers—even though their minds might wander. ■

DRAW SIMPLE SHAPES

If you've ever been tempted to scrawl circle upon circle until you've covered an entire sheet of paper, you've already mastered one great doodle-fidget method: drawing simple shapes. From squares to straight lines, triangles to rectangles—it doesn't make much difference what your polygons look like—any shape that gets your hand moving helps improve your memory. What makes shape doodling a positive method of fidgeting is that it requires very little in terms of resources, yet it engages just enough mental energy to ward off daydreaming.

When you're scribbling shapes, your mind isn't focused on the quality or the accuracy of what you're drawing. Instead, it's focused on the content of what you're hearing. The circles you scrawl in the corner of your notepad highlight moments of a discussion or meeting—looking back at them, you'll often be able to recall exactly what was being said at that moment in which you drew a certain shape. The circles popping up in the margins of your to-do list may remind you that you need to buy laundry detergent, and the vertical rectangles you sketched along the edges of your math class scratch paper may link to a formula you've been trying to memorize. It sounds a bit wacky, but studies have shown this strategy can work wonders for the fading brain—give shape doodling a try! ■

COMBINE WORDS WITH SCRIBBLES
TO CREATE INFO-DOODLES

When you look back on your past doodles, you may find that you subconsciously pulled together both visual images and complete words without even realizing it. We call these results "info-doodles," and they make an excellent fidgeting technique for retaining new information. When in the midst of a lesson, presentation, or training, grab your pen and take notes as you normally would. As your mind begins to wander, allow yourself to start doodling whatever comes to mind. Give yourself the freedom to run wild, scribbling squiggly lines or a shoreline being invaded by an encroaching ocean. Then, when your ears capture another important concept, return to traditional note-taking. Jot down items the speaker seems to be emphasizing, like "California Coastal Commission 1972," "Gutenberg printing," or "iambic pentameter." Whenever the urge to doodle reappears, start scribbling away again.

Infusing notes with doodled images is called abstract doodling by some fidget researchers. Trying to stay focused on the entirety of a lecture or lesson requires your brain to resist extraneous urges, which actually consumes significant energy. Instead, allow yourself to give in to those doodling tendencies, and your brain will be free to pay better attention. Info-doodles help you see concepts in visual ways while also using words and more traditional note formats for step-by-step understanding. It's the best of both worlds! ■

KEEP YOUR HANDS AND FINGERS MOVING

From fidget spinners and attention-grabbing gadgets to pens and paper clips, fidgeting with your hands and fingers is a great way to focus your mind by allowing your body to channel distraction without giving in to it. Grab the object of your choice and move it in whatever way feels natural. You can:

- Squeeze a balled-up piece of paper
- Pull on a rubber band or stretchy hair tie
- Uncap and recap a pen
- Rub a smooth stone
- Push the buttons on your calculator
- Flip, tie, and twirl the dangling strings of your hooded jacket
- Unplug and plug in your laptop charger

Fidgeting with an object in your hands helps you work out the antsy feelings that come with trying to sit quietly and get work done. Any fidgety object, whether spun, clicked, pushed, or bent with your fingers, will do the trick. By touching and moving the item in your hand, you'll play out your desire to move while focusing your visual attention on whatever lies before you. The distracting thoughts that cloud your focus will be redirected to the movement of your fingers, essentially turning them into background noise and freeing your mind to concentrate on what's most important! ■

BOUNCE ON AN EXERCISE BALL

Add an exercise ball to your workspace and swap your traditional desk chair out for the ball when you need the highest levels of concentration and focus. When you sit upright atop the ball, the challenge of trying to balance yourself as you work, study, or learn will get you moving and fidgeting. Once you've mastered your balance, you can roll forward and backward or lightly bounce up and down to get that concentration flowing. Every second you sit on this bouncy ball, your body's core and your brain will both have to work to maintain your balance and keep you still, providing a subtle distraction for your unconscious mind that keeps you focused and engaged.

Where the average desk chair requires you to sit in a single position for hours, an exercise ball gives you the freedom to bounce and balance. Sitting in a chair can cause you to slouch, to scrunch yourself into odd stationary positions just to get comfortable—and there's no way your focus will stay strong when you can't even get comfortable. Researchers who study the effects of furniture in educational environments have discovered that when we're free to bounce and roll while sitting, our attention and time management improve.

Grab an exercise ball of your own and get bouncing—or just try to sit as still as you can manage—and you'll be able to work faster and keep your focus for longer periods of time. ∎

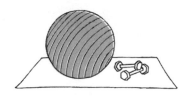

MAKE A FIST

Over the course of the workday, as in the later stages of a long project, attention can wane significantly. With that loss of attention comes a loss of memory, as the energy required to keep your body still and your mind focused exhausts your resources. To improve your ability to recall information while you work, make a fist. Clench your dominant hand tightly into a fist, especially while working with material that needs to be remembered—a series of numbers, facts, or even a speech. Hold that fist, muscles clenched, for 45 seconds before releasing. When you need to recall that crucial data later in the day, make a tight fist with your non-dominant hand. Again, hold it tight for 45 seconds.

The effect of making a fist while working is similar to grabbing and squeezing a stress ball, according to researchers. Clenching your hands, holding them closed, then slowly opening them channels your energy into the physical movement of your fingers and your muscles. Studies show that making a fist improves focus and retention, and repeating the gesture on the opposite side of the body aids recall. Additional research indicates that, if you want to change your thinking patterns, clenching each of your hands one at a time, using just the right or the left, can bring surprising results. ■

HOLD A STANDING MEETING (OR, JUST STAND)

The next time you're asked to take a seat and attend a meeting, opt to stand rather than sit. Meetings, while necessary, are both a time suck and a distraction, pulling us away from our own workload and demanding participation, focus, and creativity. Standing during a meeting, according to researchers, increases group participation, spurs creativity, and improves individual employee performance.

A standing meeting allows you the freedom to move: to sway subtly, move your hands around, lean against a wall—all of which channel your brain's energy into a positive and quiet release for better concentration. And don't limit your standing to meetings alone: stand up while getting together with your friends for increased interpersonal engagement. Rise to your feet while debating the layout plans for your new store. You can even get a new perspective by standing during a solo brainstorming session at home.

When everyone in a room stands, people are more likely to engage with one another. It's like being given the okay to interact and move. Standing while working or while in a group also boosts creativity and problem-solving skills. In addition to being an energy outlet, standing allows you to move around in a physical space, quite literally generating different views and different ideas. The new perspective you gain by standing rather than sitting literally helps you see problems and concepts from entirely new vantage points. ■

MAKE A MIND MAP

When you need to think your way through something tricky, or pay attention to a complex concept, map it out! A mind map is an easy way to turn thoughts and ideas into visualizations, helping you more clearly develop grand ideas and see new possibilities. The process is almost like outlining, as you want to include both the central, significant ideas that go to the heart of the concept and the details that add up along the way.

Begin by drawing out your main idea in the center of the paper. Then, continue by:

- Drawing lines, or branches, that stem out from the main idea
- Decorate those branches with creative thoughts and ideas—and don't be afraid to use images and pictures
- Write keywords that represent those ideas beneath the branches
- Add color, highlighting, or shading in different branches that are good ideas, weak ideas, or ideas you need to revisit

Both visual and a bit physical in its fidgeting style, a mind map brings concepts to life so you can see them broadly and in ways that are a bit more unexpected. We're used to seeing words written down as a form of explanation; images, on the other hand, can literally help with our visualization and our ability to process information. Talking or writing about grand ideas on a grand scale can easily lead to distraction—your mind wanders, you stop paying attention, and you turn to daydreaming more easily. When you can visually watch the discussion happen before you on paper, in a physical form and flow, your energy can instead be expended by examining the imagery and colors, which make almost any concept more memorable. ■

TAKE A TRIP TO DELIVER MESSAGES OR EMAILS

Before you hit "send" on yet another email or pick up the phone to call your nearby coworker, stop and stand up. Instead of relying on technology to deliver updates, gain information, or ask questions, see if you can turn your message or question into a fidget and go deliver it in person. These brief walks and moments of movement improve your focus and task performance. Sure, it's simple to send an email or chat via instant messaging systems, but getting up and discussing that very same content spurs energy, interpersonal engagement, and improved efficiency.

According to Florida State University sports scientist Jack Groppel, delivering your messages and holding in-person conversations is the perfect way to work physical movement into your long, dull tasks. Groppel found that the act of physically seeking out information is similar to athletes' quick recovery breaks during workouts. A short, sporadic movement like getting up from your desk chair (or even your couch) stimulates blood flow throughout the body, sending a flush of oxygen to the brain and leaving behind a boost of energy and fresh focus.

Of course, this fidget won't work in every case, and written communication has its place. But the next time you have just a quick question or comment to share, try taking a walk to a coworker's cubicle to refresh your attention span. ■

KNIT OR CROCHET WHILE THINKING OR TALKING

Pick up a new hobby or hone an old favorite by working with your hands as you focus on a project. Knitting and crocheting have stood the test of time as activities that keep the hands and mind sharp. Experienced knitters are quick to acknowledge that moving their needles repetitively, twisting yarn around their fingers, and following the feeling of familiar stitches is calming too. Both knitting and crocheting involve the tying of identical knots, or knot patterns, over and over, requiring very little thought as the hands move back and forth almost effortlessly.

Experts say that making something physical with your hands boosts creative thinking because a number of different senses are working all at once. For example, crocheting a scarf involves touch, sound, and sight but doesn't require an intense focus on what your hands are doing. Incorporate knitting or crocheting into your day by:

- Knitting granny squares while you chat on the phone
- Crocheting a baby blanket during a Skype meeting or conversation with a friend
- Crafting with your knitting needles as you read emails, an important document, or a new book
- Working up a crochet pattern during a family discussion about plans for an upcoming trip
- Putting your fingers in motion by knitting as you take an online class ■

PRACTICE CONSCIOUS LEG BOUNCING AND BOBBING

Sitting in a single spot for hours on end can be as tiresome as staring at the same project for long periods, and staying comfortable can require a lot of leg moving, bouncing, and bobbing. In addition to helping you find the perfect new sitting position, bobbing your legs at different speeds and in different patterns leads to improved accuracy and concentration. UC Davis professor Julie Schweitzer examined the effect of leg movement on attention and task performance, finding a clear connection between leg fidgeting and focus. Participants wore activity monitors on their ankles to track movement: individuals who sat perfectly still performed more poorly on tests requiring great concentration. Those who moved their legs (in almost any way) scored significantly better, marking correct answers more often and working faster. Leg movement also led to improved accuracy on timed tests.

Get your legs fidgeting for better focus by bouncing and bobbing in the following ways:

- Bouncing one bent leg up and down, then switching legs
- Swinging your legs from side to side, individually or together
- Bobbing each leg up and down, using the floor to push off
- Crossing one leg over the other and bouncing your leg upward and downward
- Sitting cross-legged, folding your legs up onto your chair or on the floor, so you can bounce both knees and both feet simultaneously ■

KEEP A RANDOM THOUGHT NOTEPAD

Jotting down notes during meetings, lectures, and conversations is a great way to hone your attention and focus—except when what your brain wants to scribble is a bunch of disparate thoughts with no connection to the subject at hand. Instead of giving in to the false choice of losing your ideas versus losing all interest in what's being discussed around you, write your ideas down on a special notepad meant for just these kinds of random thoughts. Whether you suddenly remembered you need to call your doctor or you just wondered how horses fall asleep, write it down. Jotting these ideas, reminders, or wandering thoughts down on paper is mindless enough to keep you focused and free of distraction, yet also ensures you don't miss out on a fantastic idea. These random thoughts are particularly helpful when you're trying to solve a tricky problem; giving life to "distracting" ideas can lead you to genius solutions you didn't consider.

You can also use your random thought notepad while you perform tasks solo. Keep a blank pad of paper nearby as you fold laundry, read your favorite monthly magazines, or sort through your email inbox. As thoughts or ideas unrelated to the task at hand pop into your head, jot them down on your pad. Looking back on those random ideas and spur-of-the-moment thoughts can help you discover interconnected threads that you can use as inspiration in the future. ■

MOVE TO A SPECIALLY DESIGNATED SPOT

A change of scenery counts as a way to fidget! When you head to a general "focus area" or even a task-specific space—like a reading chair or math workspace—you give your mind a mini-recharge. According to experts, physically leaving a space in which you were growing bored or distracted hits the reset button on your brain and attention span. When you enter the new room or area, you'll be approaching tasks from another perspective, surrounding yourself with different scenery to change your point of view and keep your level of focus up.

Another way to make this fidget work is to designate a special space for work, creative thinking, or special activities. It could be as simple as moving away from your desk to your couch or from your bedroom to your dining room. You could also create a space that includes "distracting" fidget features like vision boards, pictures, equipment, tools, or anything that you need. Add a comfy chair to do your daydreaming in, or cover your work surface in all the necessities required for organizing your recipes or designing and decorating. Any time you feel yourself waning or need a burst of focus, head into this special area. Likewise, leave the space when you complete a task to maintain its special concentration-boosting power. Make sure the space you create or choose is a physically distinct one, though; simply turning to a different corner of your desk won't result in an effective fidget. ■

PUSH, KICK, AND PLAY WITH AN EXERCISE BAND

Exercise bands are stretchy, bouncy, and fun to manipulate—they're also an excellent fidget-friendly addition to your favorite chair. Tie an exercise band between the two front legs of your chair, or stretch the band around all four legs for added tension. Have a chair with rollers? You can tie one end of an exercise band—or hook one end of a bungee cord—around the central leg of your chair, attach the other end to a leg of your desk or table, and bounce away. Just be conscious not to roll too far from your workspace! Fidget by pushing your legs backward against the stretchy band, or alternate legs as you kick and bounce against the rubbery material. You can slip your feet behind the band and press your ankles forward as well.

Leg fidgeting with an exercise band keeps your movements both silent and out of sight. Every time you kick, pull, or push, you'll reap the benefits of increased focus, improved attention to detail, and greater accuracy while working. Use this foot fidget as you read, as you chat with a friend or coworker, or while balancing your bank accounts and working with numbers. Any seated task can be better performed when your feet are fidgeting away, bouncing against a band and drumming up physical movement that excites and invigorates the brain. ■

GET PHYSICAL WHILE READING

Reading is almost made to make restless minds wander: a long, immersive, concentration-heavy activity that requires focus on every word, detail, and theme, reading is something we're taught to do while remaining silent and still. Instead of sitting quietly and training your eyes on a block of text, get up and move around the next time you read. Pace around your living room as you hold an article, walk in circles while reading a packing list or novel, hop on the treadmill at the gym to read your emails, or step from side to side in front of your desk at work. Combining reading of any kind with movement lets those feelings of distraction work their way out while your attention and engagement with a text increases.

In recent years, teachers throughout the United States have implemented different forms of movement for reading periods and have seen students' progress, engagement, and comprehension improve. Some elementary school counselors allow students to hop on exercise bikes and ride while reading. Kindergarten teachers in Kentucky encourage their students to move to music, while at least one Georgia teacher has students walk around while reading. Each of these approaches has the potential to sustain interest in reading for longer periods. ∎

SCRIBBLE SUMMARIES AND BIG PICTURE THOUGHTS

If you're not quite a skilled doodling artist but you lose focus when attempting to write down notes verbatim, adopt a method of fidgeting that's a blend of doodling and transcribing. Focus on distilling and summarizing the big picture ideas or points of a conversation or meeting. Approach the material you're hearing like someone who doesn't have time for every little detail and just jot down the broad overview. You can also make notes about how those big ideas could be implemented or why they matter, applying them while the content is still being discussed. For example, while taking notes about every symbol in a Harry Potter novel, scribble in some summaries of larger story arcs and main characters' roles. Or, rather than transcribing the details of how to speak before large audiences, track ideas that connect to related concepts instead, like different settings where confidence is beneficial.

Researchers have found that looking at both the details and the larger perspective of a process, project, or concept leads to better understanding and stronger thought connections. Considering the big picture switches the mind from consuming information to accepting new material and finding ways to apply it immediately. This note-taking approach spurs creative thought and encourages the mind to wander, making it a fidget that engages the body—in the writing itself—and the brain. ∎

TALK WITH YOUR HANDS

Gesturing while talking is often thought of as a nervous quirk, but it's actually a very productive way to fidget. Putting your hands into motion helps you express your thoughts, gives your creativity a boost, and utilizes multiple senses, all without distracting you from the larger message. The gesturing focuses your brain on your train of thought, keeping your eyes, thoughts, and attention from wandering. Researchers have also found that those who use their left hand to gesture generate more creative, innovative thoughts compared to those who use only their right hand, and left-hand gesturing can help individuals see problems from different perspectives—so make your left hand move just as much as your right!

Connect with the speaking power of your hands. Try incorporating the following hand movements into your conversations:

- Perform identical gestures with both hands simultaneously
- Use your left hand to accentuate important points or to add impact to certain words
- Gesture toward those listening with one hand, inviting them into your statements and remarks
- Point your finger toward any nearby props or examples
- Make a list, spelling out and punctuating each number with your fingers
- Demonstrate sizes by gesturing upward or across your body with both hands ■

WIGGLE YOUR TOES

Feel like you're about to nod off over the stove? Can't keep track of the conversation happening around you as your ears tune out others' voices? When you feel your attention span slipping, start moving your toes. Wiggle your toes up, down, in any direction as long as you can feel those digits moving inside your shoes. Focus your mind on that small, imperceptible movement and pay close attention to the feeling. Are your toes squished together and touching one another? Is there a rhythm you can wiggle away to? Is it difficult to wiggle some toes but not others? A quick toe wiggle will bring you back from the verge of distraction and make you a more effective listener.

Wiggling your toes is a smart public fidget because it isn't distracting to others. Although it's a fidget only you know about, it's still incredibly helpful when your focus wanes. Experts have found that this small movement encourages attentiveness. Often, the world around us demands concentration on multiple fronts—from the ping of a new email to an instant message to a phone call—lessening our ability to focus on what's most important. When we find ourselves in environments that aren't exciting or stimulating, our attention often starts to wander. Wiggling your toes is a simple way to excite the mind and get back on track. ■

GET UP AND LIE DOWN

We all desperately wish we could lie down and take a catnap in the middle of a challenging, lackluster, or tiresome task. Lying down on the job is definitely likely to get you marked as lazy and unproductive—unless everyone knows you're lying on the floor to fidget your way to new ideas and improved focus! A study conducted by researchers at the Australian National University discovered that people become better problem-solvers while lying down compared to when they are sitting normally. When prone, subjects were both faster and more accurate at solving anagrams and visual problems. Other research found that lying down spurs creativity and focus, allowing subjects to achieve deeper focus by changing their perspective from upright to supine. Stop staring at your computer screen, textbook, or television and lie on the floor to reinvigorate your brain, your perspective, and your focus. Just make sure you check in with the boss first!

While lying down on the floor during an all-office meeting or a party-planning session with a group of your friends may not be perceived as productive, doing so on your own time (in the confines of your own space, of course) is a smart way to fidget. Sprawl out on the floor during your next brainstorming session or when you're trying to find a solution to a tricky puzzle. Take a few minutes to lie down while working on a project, assignment, or task that requires insight, like organization, creative writing, or a crossword puzzle, and your relaxing fidgeting style might lead to a creative breakthrough! ∎

ROLL, OR EXERCISE, YOUR EYES

Give your sight and your mind a break by rolling your eyes. According to the results of research published in *Brain and Cognition*, people who move their eyes right and left increase their original thinking, produce more creative ideas, and spur communication between the two sides of the brain. Research participants were asked to list alternative uses for everyday items such as paper clips and pencils in just 60 seconds. When researchers asked the participants to move their eyes horizontally and then return to the same task, the fidgety movements led to a significant increase in the generation of new ideas.

To boost your creativity, generate new ideas, and think outside the box, fidget with your eyeballs. Roll your eyes simultaneously, moving them from left to right and right to left. You can also move your eyes back and forth from side to side, and you'll get creative thoughts flowing without losing focus on the work before you. Use this easy eye fidget to think of names for your new pet, create a list of unique approaches to your wedding seating chart, or devise new methods of keeping your piles of paperwork organized. Keep in mind that tracing your gaze from side to side is the best method for connecting the two hemispheres of the brain. ∎

PERFORM A BRAIN DUMP

Every day our brains are filled with tasks to complete, rules to follow, problems to solve, and more, all of which drain our energy and our focus. Somewhat similar to doodling the random images and thoughts that run through your brain, a brain dump is meant to help clear your mind and boost your creativity.

A brain dump is a quick, productive fidget that empties the mind for better concentration and cognitive performance. All you have to do is freely write random ideas.

Also referred to as free association, a brain dump is performed by writing down every thought that comes to mind. Don't worry about revising what you scrawl, or about spelling, grammar, or even making sense. Just write and write and let your brain run wild. Once you've emptied all of your thoughts onto paper, take a look at what you came up with. You'll probably notice trends, connections, or even great ideas hidden in the ramblings you wrote down. You may even discover new perspectives and solutions, like the answer to managing a crazy daily schedule or the reason why your newest recipe hasn't panned out perfectly! ■

TAP YOUR FEET

In the course of working on a long project, you'll probably feel like giving up at some point even though your schedule won't allow it. This is the perfect time to move your feet and channel those jittery, potentially frustrated feelings into an outlet!

Moving your feet to the beat helps focus your mind on the task at hand, improve cognition, and eliminate the distractions that can cause thoughts to wander. Tapping and bouncing your extremities balances intense concentration with a release of physical energy. Bounce the heels of your feet up and down as you pull together those travel plans, tap your toes secretly inside your shoe while you try to piece together a month's worth of daily menus, or stomp at the floor softly when you're immersed in data entry for hours on end.

If that isn't enough reason to tap along to your favorite playlist or jiggle your legs while typing away, there's an added health benefit too. Research has found that people who tap their feet while seated improve their cardiovascular health, get blood flowing through the body, and keep their arteries healthy. So, in addition to providing stimulation and firing up the brain, every foot tap fidgets your body down the path to better health. ■

PART 2

SIGHT

FIDGETING WITH VISUAL DETAILS

Admit it: you've been caught staring out the windows of the conference room or at your lap during a presentation. When you find yourself lost in thought, you aren't necessarily distracted from what's in front of you: we fidget with our eyes too. That glazed-over look or distracted, off-in-space stare is often a way of improving your attention span, even if it looks or even feels like an attempt to escape into another world.

Visual fidgeting is all about sensation, according to psychologists. While you may not be physically feeling or moving your way to better concentration and productivity, you're using the visual details of your surrounding environment to stimulate your brain. For example, sitting in a bare gray cubicle can dull anyone's drive and motivation, making it more challenging to stay energetic and productive through the long workday. Yet introduce a bit of color or movement—a window, for example, or a work of art—and a small hum of activity livens up the brain, providing inspiration and increased stimulation. Everyone has his or her own preferred work environment, yet we often surrender to whatever is standard and mass-produced. Give your eyes something to feast on, however, and you'll find yourself getting more things done.

If you ever feel trapped at your desk, in a classroom, or during a meeting, you aren't alone. When people are restricted to a visually numbing environment and expected to concentrate, they often report high levels of both mental activity and distraction—lots of thoughts, usually not relevant to the work at hand. That's where fidgeting with your eyes can help. Researchers from the University of Illinois at Urbana-Champaign studied the effect of a visual sight "break" on students sitting in a classroom. Students who had a view through a window to the outside world performed considerably better on tests; they achieved improved information recall and lower stress levels. Researchers at the University of Melbourne found similar results in a study examining the effects of 40-second "microbreaks": subjects who spent 40 seconds staring at a picture of greenery boosted their focus, improved their attention span, and performed at a higher level when they returned to their work.

Sight fidgeting helps you get into a focused frame of mind, calms your anxious feelings, and restores concentration. Visual fidgets can be meditative and mindful, stimulating or soothing. Looking around the room or out a window is also found to improve listening skills and enhance group discussions—plus it's much less distracting to those around you than most forms of physical fidgeting. Don't be afraid to let your eyes wander. Forget about keeping your line of sight on the whiteboard, paper, or computer screen before you. Wandering eyes and a change of scenery can do wonders for your attentiveness and productivity.

MAKE YOUR WRITING UTENSILS COLORFUL

Drop the traditional (and boring!) black or blue pen the next time you need to write something out by hand. Instead, choose some new colors for your writing utensils and turn the act of writing into a sensory, visual form of fidgeting. Whether taking notes, conducting research, or writing out instructions, employing a variety of colors improves mental recall, increases productivity, and leads to better work performance.

Typically we write in one color. That means that when you look back at your notes, all you see is a blur of identical-looking text, all in the same shape, color, and style. Adding color brings a punch of life to any written material.

The different colors stand out, drawing your attention to different areas of the notes—and, more importantly, the content becomes more memorable. You'll remember that the blue ink represented one speaker's ideas, while red marks a series of crucial to-do items, for example. Swapping colors while writing helps the content stick in your brain better and makes the act of rereading the notes easier.

Adopt this colorful sight fidget by doing any of the following:

- Switch between different-colored writing utensils for different kinds of ideas
- Alternate from green to red ink to make important ideas stand out
- Use colorful highlighters to mark different types of information, such as dates in purple and names in pink
- Use a blue highlighter to distinguish between facts you're struggling to memorize and those you already know well
- Mark different events or occasions on your calendar in different-colored ink ■

LOSE YOURSELF IN A BUSY WINDOW SCENE

Are you constantly drawn to the nearest window while working? Do you swivel in your chair just so you can check out the activity on the streets below? Are you prone to staring out at a park or even a parking lot, just to change up your line of sight? Keep doing it! Any time you need to visually fidget in the midst of tackling projects that dull your focus, directing your attention toward a window is a handy fidget. Stare freely out and concentrate on nothing more than the busy activity of people walking, cars driving, or animals roaming.

Referred to as Attention Restoration Theory by some researchers, the act of simply looking out a window gives the brain a short break and moment of relief. When we're trying to complete an activity that requires all of our focus and attention, we grow mentally exhausted—and this is even more likely to occur if a task is both cognitively demanding and utilizes repetitive skills and motions. To relieve that exhaustion, a window provides a visual fidgeting opportunity that reinvigorates. Students who are able to look out of windows while working in the classroom improve their academic performance. In the workplace, staring at an outdoor space restores and reanimates your mental energy—it even lowers stress. ■

VISUALLY "PLAY" WITH WATER OR SAND

Water and sand toys are captivating and an excellent way to fidget without moving anything more than your eyes. Often shunned by teachers and managers, toys that allow water and sand to run through a series of fun obstacles are indeed easy to dismiss as silly distractions, but their distracting qualities are exactly what makes them a perfect sight fidget! Visually captivating and hands-free, a water or sand timer allows part of your mind to concentrate on something other than your workload, which leads to rejuvenation and restored focus.

Put a water or sand timer on your desk and allow yourself the freedom to gaze at it anytime the urge arises. Watch these "distracting" devices until the timer ends, then return to your work. Focus your eyes on:

- The single blue drops of liquid dripping from one spinning wheel to the next
- The slow onslaught of sand trickling from the upper half of an hourglass
- The splash of colorful liquid as it reaches the bottom of the timer
- The spinning wheels or raising and lowering levers moved by the water or sand

Watching sand slip through an hourglass or liquid spin along brightly colored wheels enhances productivity and relieves stress during work. Research has found that restless individuals need a new type of visual stimulation beyond the computer screen to release pent-up worry and spur creativity. Watch a water or sand timer and you can clear your mind, bring on fresh new thoughts, and improve learning. ■

STARE OFF INTO SPACE

Go ahead, stare off into space. When you turn your attention away from the computer screen you've been laboring at all morning, you're doing your focus and your eyes a world of good. Called "microbreaks" or "visual breaks," these periods of staring at absolutely nothing are smart visual fidgets that refresh the mind, reduce eye stress, and get you back on task. Feel free to stare at anything that isn't directly in front of you. Glance at the ceiling, stare at the carpet, or look far ahead at something on the walls. As long as it's something new, your brain and attention span will soon reset.

Researchers recommend turning and looking at something far away for the following lengths of time:

- 15 seconds to reduce fatigue
- 30 seconds to improve mental acuteness
- 5 minutes to give your eyes a break
- 15 minutes to increase productivity

Trying to focus your attention on a single activity for hours upon hours becomes both boring and difficult as the day wears on. Your mind will inevitably start to wander, so keep yourself on task, better motivated, and less exhausted by incorporating staring breaks into your routine as a visual fidget. Breaking the workday into these short components helps concentration and results in better quality work too. Do your attention span a favor and stop staring at your current project for just a few seconds, no matter how much stress you're under. ▪

VISUALIZE THE CONCEPT, PROBLEM, OR TASK WHILE WORKING

Go ahead and get some shut-eye at your desk while working hard; just don't let yourself slip into actual dreams! Instead, when you feel your attention waning, close your eyes and visualize the concept, problem, or goal you're working on. Redraw your work in visual representations or drum up images of related items and concepts to make the ideas clearer in your mind. Visualize:

- The moment you'll hand your boss the completed presentation
- The number line, with negatives on one end and positives on the other
- Piecing together a puzzle
- Fitting the small pieces of a model perfectly in place
- The act of implementing new software
- An image of the moon or spaceships when trying to remember the events of 1968

Scientific research has shown that associating visual imagery with facts you need to remember or steps you need to take is an effective memory tool. Especially if you work more often with numbers and words than you do with images, visual fidgeting improves focus and information retention. It's another way to view information in a nontraditional, word-free format. Give yourself a break and fidget with your visual imagination to get yourself motivated to dive back into the work at hand. ■

GIVE YOURSELF COLOR-CODED FEEDBACK

There's a reason teachers use the famed-and-dreaded red pen when editing, correcting, and grading student work. Red stands out against black ink and offers a visual contrast between your contributions and their feedback. Adopt that same color-coded method for your own work, and provide yourself with a method of visual fidgeting that improves productivity, speeds up efficiency, and makes poring over documents a lot easier. Nicknamed "color-coded feedback," the practice of using color to edit and leave comments helps guide the eyes directly to what requires immediate attention.

Become your own editor by grabbing a red (or any other colored) pen and get correcting, rearranging, or underlining. Essentially, you want to maximize the amount of color you use to guide yourself through the steps of a project. Write out the steps you need to follow on brightly colored sticky notes—for example, use pink for urgent, purple for final touches, and green for problem areas. Or, revise your email to a client by leaving comments for yourself in blue or red. This visual feedback will train your eyes on what needs work and make it easier to determine what you need to do next. ■

STARE INTO A FLAME
(OR, WATCH A VIDEO OF A LIT FIREPLACE)

If you need to reinvigorate your attention and energy, or you feel yourself growing bored at your desk, placate the urge to quit by looking at a burning fire. There likely isn't a fireplace readily available in your office or workspace of course, but all you need is an online video of a roaring, cozy fire to allow yourself the space to visually fidget. As the fire burns, concentrate on how the flames move and appear. Zone in on the different colors at the tip of each flame, the blends of red, yellow, and deep orange. Follow the sparks and licks of the fire, watching as it moves, waves, and jumps. Allow yourself to stare at every little aspect, change, and motion. See if you can identify shapes within the depths of the flames, watching for slight shifts and features or faces.

Whether in person or via video, staring at flames or fire offers soothing relaxation and provides a release for your pent-up, fidget-driven energy. Rather than keeping your eyes on the dull material awaiting your attention, you give yourself a visual break that allows your eyes to wander onto something new. As you pay attention to the fire, you'll also let your mind run free and become distracted by something entirely new. A few minutes of this fidget and you'll be refreshed and mentally strong, ready to dive back in. ∎

USE A WEIRD, UNUSUAL FONT

Fonts matter. The world traditionally relies on just a few typical font styles for important documents and communication. Buck tradition and fidget your way to a better attention span by typing and reading in weird, wacky, and different fonts. Start typing your documents in a font that's curly, elegant, dramatic—any style that's drastically different from those you see on a regular basis. It doesn't matter what size or style; your only goal should be to choose a font that's hard-—yes, hard!—to read.

Some commonly available font formats or styles that are rarely used in documents, reading material, and online correspondence include:

- Typewriter styles
- Script-based fonts with scrolling curves and linked letters
- Rounded letter styles
- Fonts with larger spaces between each character
- Large and bold typefaces

While the goal of sticking with traditional font families makes text more universally easy to read, that simplicity doesn't do a thing for focus or productivity. In fact, reading something in Times New Roman can even distract you as your eyes become bored, making you less likely to remember what exactly you read. Researchers have found that reading material in unusual fonts is incredibly helpful if you hope to better remember content, facts, and important material. When trying to read a more challenging, unfamiliar font, you have to concentrate harder and devote more attention to understand what you're reading. That greater focus and emphasis on the material often results in improved retention. ■

LOOK AT SOMETHING GREEN AND NATURE-BASED

Does your environment feature at least one window with a sweeping view of the great outdoors? If there's a space of green or nature that you can stare at, use that window view as a scenic fidget. When you feel yourself drawn to distraction or your energy starting to wane before the chores in front of you are complete, turn your line of sight toward nature. Look out the window and examine the grass, the trees, the blossoms, the bushes. Taking a few seconds, even a full minute, to gaze out at some greenery results in improved work performance, stress relief, and better focus. Take in the sights of nature, even if you have to fake it with a plastic plant or a false window scene.

Researchers studied what happens to students who absentmindedly stare out windows while attending class. After comparing kids who stared at outdoor scenes to those who kept their attention on the teacher alone, the researchers found that gazing at nature equated to better test performance, attention to class material, and recovery from stress. A quick look out the window restores mental stamina without any distraction at all. Nature doesn't often make it indoors and into our offices or classrooms, but it provides a huge boost in regard to fidgeting. If you don't have a great view of nature, adopt this form of fidgeting by bringing a live, green plant into your living room or looking at a picture of a landscape online to reap similar benefits. ▪

TAKE A PHOTO BREAK

As mentioned previously, a quick glance at a picture of a landscape can provide the same benefits as looking through a window to the outdoors. When faced with a task or lesson that requires complex thought and careful attention, give yourself quick 30-second breaks during which you look at an image of something outdoorsy. View a sloping green hill, a park, or a bird's nest; any nature-based image will do. Put the picture away once the time is up, and you'll find yourself ready to dive back into work—even if the task is tedious.

Turning to a visual, sight-based fidget technique during particularly exhausting and demanding work is a fantastic method for improving focus and work performance. Because our days are typically spent indoors, far away from the great outdoors and its refreshing qualities, introducing a new view and a new image that's different from our surroundings brings the perfect interruption or distraction. Take a quick look at a picture of a beautiful plant or a winter wonderland, and you'll perform better for the remainder of the workday. ■

WATCH A FISH TANK

Fish tanks contain fabulous underwater scenes, with fish swimming, bubbles bubbling, and scenic plants wavering in the controlled environment. They're also an excellent method of sight fidgeting, because they provide a ton of activity in exchange for nothing more than your gaze for a few minutes. Check out any fish tank, large and expansive or tiny and featuring just a few fish. Pay attention to the shimmering light as it catches fishes' fins; look closely at the artificial decorations, the way fish dart around or under the structures; watch the creatures' fins wiggle and move. Or, think about nothing at all and allow your vision to be transfixed by whatever happens before your eyes as the fish move through the tank. Let the fish tank scene consume all of your attention and focus for a few minutes whenever you're feeling distracted, tired, and unmotivated.

According to researchers at Plymouth University and the University of Exeter, watching a fish tank and its underwater world offers great cognitive benefits. Watching the tank leads to decreases in both blood pressure and heart rate, creates mood improvement, and supports calm. That's why fish tanks are so often present in workplaces and doctor's offices: they're calming and intriguing, and just a few seconds' glance is beneficial. Distract yourself with a colorful fish tank, and you'll return to your workload a bit happier and more refreshed. ∎

LOSE YOURSELF IN MEMES AND CUTE ANIMALS

If you're tempted throughout the day to turn to your smartphone and swipe through hilarious memes and adorable puppy pictures, don't feel bad about "wasting time" by doing so. The more memes you laugh at and the more pictures of cute kittens you view—within reason, of course—the more productive you'll be. Stimulate your brain by visually fidgeting with distracting images of funny, enjoyable pictures. Browse your favorite political memes, view a series of cat pictures, and stare at entertaining images from your *Instagram* feed. Spend a few minutes checking out your favorite famous pets and getting lost in the cuteness. You'll likely return to any task, whether grocery shopping, completing homework, or tackling a slew of survey questions, happier as a result. In addition to bringing a smile to your face, there's a scientific reason your brain will benefit.

Science supports this sight-based method of fidgeting: researchers in Japan found that looking at adorable animal pictures boosts productivity. After viewing pictures of fluffy chicks, swimming otters, and typical cats and dogs, subjects felt positive emotions that led them to feel more motivated and more ready to approach difficult tasks. The pictures also improved workers' systematic processing capabilities. Taking a few moments to distract yourself from your work by looking at images that bring a smile to your face will make you a better employee, more dedicated and more likely to ward off boredom as it arises. ∎

LOOK AT THE CLEANEST, NEATEST AREA OF YOUR WORKSPACE

Do you like to work in the midst of a mess, surrounded by piles and not bothered by a little disorganization? Or do you prefer a tidy, organized space that's free from any disarray? Clutter may not be distracting to everyone, but a bare and clean workspace can be the better of the two options. Clean work areas have long been touted by both parents and productivity experts as the best environments in which to work—just looking at something organized and neat can be a form of fidgeting too.

When you're feeling distracted, look away from the mess at your desk and instead stare at the cleanest, most clutter-free area in sight. A neat space inspires focus, literally clearing the clutter from your mind and giving you a blank slate. It'll essentially wipe away the anxious, tedious feelings you have after facing your workload for hours.

Take a minute and stare at a clean space, and you'll improve your focus as well as your productivity. The best method of enhancing productivity is to give part of yourself free rein to run wild, and with a blank, clean space before your eyes, your mind will start to circle around to new thoughts. Marvel at your neatly contained and sparse space, and your mind will follow suit with renewed ability to follow a set task. ■

LET YOUR EYES ROAM YOUR MESSIEST SPACE

A clean, neat space might clear some minds, but a messy desk can also affect your brain, your focus, and your ideas. Although tidiness is often associated with productivity, it's also true that some messy desk dwellers are more creative and generate more new ideas. According to a series of studies published in the *Journal of Consumer Research*, looking at a messy environment or working in one led to clearer, simpler thinking: participants subconsciously used the mess nearby to pare down their thinking and keep their minds clear. The sight of clutter can help us block out distractions, focusing the brain on the single task before us and allowing for clearer decision-making.

If you typically surround yourself with a neat, orderly environment, make a mess—or, simply look at the messiest area you can find nearby. Gaze into the depths of your laundry room, where clothes pile up haphazardly, or stare at your kids' messy, disorganized playroom with toys strewn everywhere. Spend a few seconds looking at your roommate's room in disarray, clothing and papers covering every inch of the floor, or turn to a messy office break room with a sink full of dishes. Some fidget-savvy folks will even keep two separate workspaces, one filled with disorganization and one kept tidy and free of clutter to suit the need to fidget visually whenever it arises. Any messy setting or environment will do; the sight of disorganization will spark creative thinking and inspire you to return your full attention to whatever demands it. ■

EXPOSE YOURSELF TO ART

Draw your attention to any art near you, and don't be afraid to let your eyes and mind wander while staring. Taking in art of any kind—abstract, scenic, landscape, or even portrait—is a great visual fidget for distracted minds in need of restored focus. Turn your eyes to the art hanging on supermarket walls or on the walls of your office, and let yourself get a little lost. Stare at the intricacies or the brushstrokes. Examine the details of a scenic image, or gaze into the eyes of a striking portrait. While looking at each piece of art, you'll notice interesting and thought-provoking aspects that get your brain working and thinking in new ways. Basically, you'll be soaking in the creativity and innovative spirit of whatever artwork you gaze upon, finding your own focus in the ingenuity of another's work.

Even glancing at art boosts creative thinking, stimulates conversation, and provides an outlet for distraction. Give a quick look over at your chosen artwork when you feel boredom creeping into your mind, and you can return to your work with new insight and perspective. It's also another way to give yourself a little fidget break; just let yourself think without limitations or rules while gazing, and you'll feel freer and lighter when returning to your responsibilities. ■

FREEZE YOUR FOCUS FOR 10 SECONDS

Clear your mind, improve your comprehension, strengthen your memory, and visually fidget distractions away by stopping your work for just 10 seconds. Stop whatever you're working on or doing, lock your eyes on something in your line of sight, and count to ten. Pay close attention to whatever it is you're looking at: gaze at the bright colors of a nearby plant, watch the bumpy texture of a blank wall, or get lost in the lines of a painting. Once the 10 seconds are up, return to your task. If you have time, or need to work your way through a particularly dense, long task, you can change your visual and mental freeze from 10 seconds to a full minute.

The 10-second sight freeze is a quick meditative practice that stops distraction and unproductive thoughts from creeping in. Your mind takes a quick relaxation break, and without anything to ponder, is free to get creative. UC Santa Barbara studied the benefits of focused mindfulness and found that individuals who practiced brief meditation and mindfulness on a regular basis were tested against those who didn't—and the meditating bunch proved to have better reading comprehension, improved working memory, and fewer distraction responses. Giving yourself a 10-second freeze fights off distractions and helps you avoid losing focus, and the memory boost is helpful too. Don't forget to focus only on the present during your 10-second freezes to make certain you're making the best of it. ■

VISUALIZE THE DISTANT FUTURE
OR A FAR-OFF PLACE

Take a quick break to visually fidget by feeling, seeing, and imagining without moving a muscle. Pause what you're doing and spend a minute or two visualizing something from the future, somewhere far from home, or some kind of activity. Imagine what the streets will look like in 2175—what comes after self-driving cars? Envision your favorite faraway vacation spot, imagining the waves hitting the shore or the forest filled with sounds. Pretend you're riding a bike, hands gripping the handlebars and legs moving up and down as you balance while riding forward. Place your imagined self in outer space, exploring sights you've never even seen or experienced.

Visualizing your goals is a well-known and perhaps even necessary part of achieving those goals. Instead of visualizing what you'd like to accomplish, try a different approach by visualizing a far-off location. Research published in the *Journal of Experimental Social Psychology* connects this less common type of visualization to problem-solving abilities, creative thinking, and greater concentration. Educators, too, have found that visualizing distant places, times, and scenarios increases engagement during lectures and learning activities. Allow your mind to wander creatively, and you'll return to your work filling out spreadsheets, painting portraits, or teaching a yoga class with reinvigorated focus. ■

GAZE AT A WHITE WALL

Take a white wall break the next time distraction starts to rear its head. All you need to do is turn your attention to a wall that's free of any color, any decoration—yep, a plain white wall. Fix your eyes on the untouched surface for a few minutes. When you're ready, turn back to whatever you were working on. This form of visual fidgeting is effortless too—white walls surround us at just about every turn, at home and out in the world at large. Create your own white wall by staring at:

- A blank Word document
- A blank piece of white paper
- A whiteboard
- A length of white fabric
- A clean, mark-free white floor

Staring at a blank white space has been a helpful fidget for centuries. Artist Pablo Picasso was known to stare at white walls to drum up inspiration before he painted. Startups and innovative business leaders rely on empty whiteboards or white walls to spur creative thought as they design and develop new approaches and new technology. Innovators, creative types like writers and artists, and managers from a range of fields find that a white wall or surface improves the ability to draw connections, make new associations, and reflect on the most important parts of a task. You too can find focus, creativity, and the motivation to get working in the blank white surface of a wall. ■

DIM THE LIGHTS

Fight distraction while going through the mail or improve your creative thinking when setting your schedule by turning down the lights in whatever room you're in. Turn off your shockingly bright desk lamp, or use the dimmer switch in your dining room; you can even swap out your sunny lightbulbs for ones that produce less white light for certain tasks that need a great deal of cognitive attention. Can't control the light around you? Take a few minutes to close your eyes and pretend you're sitting in the dark, and you'll capture a bit of that same effect.

While natural light is touted as the best for vision, research has discovered that dim lighting improves creative performance and makes individuals feel more free to use their creativity. A series of studies published in the *Journal of Environmental Psychology* tested the effects of dim lighting on creativity—the results showed that those who work in dimly lit settings are more likely to be creative in their thinking and approach to tasks. Dim lighting also leads to more exploratory and open processing. If you're worried that dim lighting will pose visibility problems, researchers note that the lighting should be kept bright enough so as not to strain your eyes, but not nearly as bright as the artificial light found in most public (and even many private) spaces. ■

SWITCH BETWEEN TWO SCREENS

If you've been using two desktop screens for your computer-related tasks, you've been fidgeting without realizing it. Moving between two screens is a subtle way to fidget, keeping your focus steady and creating physical separation between your distractions and your workload. You can perfect this fidget in any of these three ways:

- Add an additional monitor to your desk or workspace. It can be placed next to your primary screen or a short distance away on the same surface.
- Utilize the multiple desktops feature on your laptop.
- Use different devices for physically separate workspaces, such as a laptop and tablet or a desktop and laptop.

All of these approaches visually change what you're focused on, helping to guide your concentration. Experts recommend that you store or move all fun, distracting features to one monitor, desktop, or device; for example, move your messaging apps, your favorite websites, and social media apps to the secondary screen. Keep your primary screen centered solely on a single task or project, like writing, inputting data, or researching. This decreases the odds that you will lose focus. When you want to give in to distraction, simply switch screens or devices and play around with your "fun" monitor. ■

PART 3

TASTE

FIDGETS WITH BITE AND SPICE

The act of chewing, snapping, or blowing bubbles with a piece of gum. The first sip of coffee. The cold, refreshing sting of a piece of ice as you suck or chew on it. All of these tastes and sensations are enjoyable, yes—but they're also often really important to our brains. These actions are all taste fidgets: the movements, chews, bites, snaps, and licks that get your mind working and back on track. Though you've probably been forced to spit out a piece of gum in class or lectured by a parent for gnawing on the eraser end of a pencil, taste-based fidgets are mentally stimulating and bring concentration benefits along with every sip and smack.

The teeth, tongue, and mouth are all related to our memory and our ability to focus. When you fidget with different parts of your mouth and taste buds, you're releasing your energy while still focusing on the task, conversation, or lesson happening around you. Chewing on a pen isn't illustrating a lack of attention; rather, it's a motion that almost physically illustrates a brain processing what it hears by "crunching" new information. Different foods and flavors, too, can shape behavior, learning ability, and information retention—so don't be afraid to snap that gum even if it slightly annoys your friends. According to researchers at Columbia University and the National Institutes of Health, the body's taste receptors impact our ability to recall memories and form new ones. Snacking while working can spur creativity, and tasting a cinnamon-flavored treat can even provide a brief energy boost to increase productivity.

Scientific research is still relatively new when it comes to taste-based fidgeting, but there's an overwhelming amount of research indicating that fidgeting-type stimulation supports learning and can provide an acceptable outlet for those who need to fidget while they work. In 2011, researchers found that the act of chewing can increase alertness, alleviate stress, and enhance cognition. The benefits of chewing and gnawing were also studied by researchers at Cardiff University, who found that these mouthy fidgeting behaviors improved concentration and improved short-term memory recall when listening. The more monotonous and lengthy the activity, the more chewing paid off. While new research will continue to discover even more about taste fidgeting, there's already evidence that putting your mouth to work when you're feeling distracted can be a big help.

While handing over a chewed-up pen to a friend or slowly chewing your way through a gooey, sticky treat may seem like unusual "thinking" behavior, those prone to taste fidgeting already know that it can get creative juices flowing and the brain thinking. Don't be afraid to chomp, chew, drink—even stick your tongue out in the midst of working or paying attention. By using your mouth and taste buds correctly, this method of fidgeting can lead to improved focus, greater attention to detail, a rush of new ideas, and, most importantly, a boost in output. Keep your mouth busy, and your brain will be awash in activity too.

CHEW A STICK OF GUM

Gum tastes good, and it's a workout for mouth and mind alike. With every chew, snap, and pull, a single stick of gum is working to improve your skill during cognitive tasks like math and writing, increase your focus, and make you more productive. Pop a piece of gum—assuming you've got the go-ahead from any observant higher-ups, of course—and get chewing when you need to work through some budgeting tasks or craft a long letter. While a single piece can give you the alertness you need, you can also chew consistently throughout the day to keep your alertness and focus consistent. Feel free to chew a stick whenever you feel a little antsy or distracted, and you can focus on the act of chewing while working.

The very first study that scientifically connected chewing gum with brain performance and focus was conducted in 1939. In the decades since, many more studies have claimed similar findings—and more recently, chewing gum as a fidget was proven to boost individuals' moods and alertness in addition to offering attention-boosting benefits. Together, scientific studies report that fidgeting via chewing gum leads to increased happiness, lower levels of job-related stress, reduced fatigue, and improved performance during challenging and demanding tasks. ∎

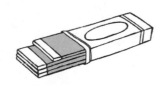

CRUNCH ICE WITH YOUR TEETH

Quick, before that ice melts! Put those frozen cubes to work for you and start chomping. Gnawing on ice cubes helps you think through complex problems while writing and performing other demanding cognitive tasks. As you fidget, you'll stop your focus from flagging and give yourself a quick concentration boost. Crunching through frozen water stimulates your focus and your productivity and is a great variation on the standard chew-fidget. If your teeth aren't up to this task, you can achieve similar effects by sucking on the cubes until they melt.

Known as "mastication-induced arousal," chewing ice or any other difficult-to-chew item sends wakeup signals to your brain, improving focus and drawing your attention to what you're trying to concentrate on. What ice lacks in taste, it makes up for by boosting your attention span and your ability to focus. Just keep in mind that this fidgeting method only provides a brief lift, meaning you'll want to use it for quick tasks or the most difficult ones rather than an all-day productivity strategy. ∎

CHEW AT YOUR LIPS OR CHEEK

High-energy people often find themselves fidgeting without even realizing it. If you tend to chew on your lips or bite your cheeks, you've already developed a helpful fidgeting habit. When focus starts to fade, chewing on your lips and cheeks evokes the gum-chewing effect, in which moving your mouth improves concentration and gives you an outlet for your energy. Even though you're working hard to stay still and on task, that chewing motion allows for a little bit of satisfying, boredom-defeating movement while you work. You can chew the edges of your lip, clench your jaw, or chomp at the skin inside your cheek; all of these fidgeting techniques have the same impact.

It's common for people to fidget by chewing their lips or the insides of their cheeks, and scientific research explains that it's not just an outlet for energy but a source of stimulation too. When we need to concentrate deeply, our brains want to use our mouths to express that thinking. By keeping the mouth moving in some manner, you're freeing up your brain to concentrate on the task because it won't have to worry about reining in your mouth or tongue. Let yourself chew, bite, and gnaw freely, and your stress levels will decrease as your attention span, response time, and productivity increase. ▪

GRAB A CHEWY, CHALLENGING SNACK

Chewing a gooey, sticky, or challenging snack while working or learning is the perfect way to fidget yourself to better alertness and productivity. Grab a sticky granola bar, a stubborn piece of toffee, tough beef jerky, or a lollipop filled with a chewable center. Any snack that requires you to work your mouth in order to enjoy it is a great fidgeting tool. As you work to eat these difficult foods, you'll develop a rhythm that keeps distraction at bay, improves your mood, and makes working more enjoyable.

The act of chewing, licking, or moving food around in your mouth will keep you calm and focused as you work on potentially difficult or frustrating problems. Your mouth is kept busy by the tricky treat and your brain doesn't have to try to control or instruct it. Instead, your mental focus can be directed solely at whatever you're working on. You'll also improve your reaction time, as your intense focus will make you better able to adapt and adjust quickly. ■

DRINK DECAF INSTEAD OF CAFFEINATED COFFEE

If you need to increase focus, coffee is a natural choice to sip on while you work, but too many trips to the coffee machine, as we all know, can make your mind wander and give you the urge to twitch in an unproductive way. (Jitters and fidgeting are not the same thing.) Opt for a hot mug of decaf instead and pretend it's caffeinated!

Using your imagination sparks the placebo effect and keeps you busy by "fidgeting" as you reach for your cup and take regular drinks. Studies show that while we assume it's the caffeine in coffee perking us up, even a cup of imaginary decaf sparks creative thinking and increases productivity. While an excess of caffeine makes the mind wander, amped up and unable to focus, a pretend cup makes you feel as though every sip is benefitting your work speed. The key is in the act of imagining what you're drinking is something entirely different. Every time you take a sip, imagine that the warm beverage is fueling your motivation, and you'll begin improving your attention right away. ■

TASTE A BIT OF MINT

Take advantage of the benefits of herbs and amp up your productivity with the taste of mint. Whether fresh or synthetic, mint-flavored foods and drinks help improve focus and fight off the boredom and sleepiness that come with a long workday. When you taste fresh mint or something filled with peppermint flavor while trying to pay attention, you're subconsciously fidgeting your way to improved information retention, better focus, and stronger cognitive function. You don't have to do anything more than bite, suck on, chew, or drink something minty; simply grab a peppermint stick, enjoy its taste, and you'll likely become more focused.

A study by Wheeling Jesuit University examined the effects of the flavor of peppermint on working people. Tasting peppermint was found to improve problem-solving skills, enhance judgment, boost the attention span, and strengthen memory skills. Researchers at Coventry University also found in a recent study that those who chewed mint gum increased their energy and felt more awake—adding benefits beyond the fidget of gum chewing alone by making mint tasters more alert. Opt for minty flavors of chewing gum, or skip the gum entirely and stick with drinking mint tea, biting a spring of fresh mint in your mouth, or snacking on mint cookies. ■

BITE YOUR PEN OR PENCIL

Your family and friends think it's gross. So what? Chewing on or biting your writing utensils is a fidget that fires up the brain, improves your mood, and alleviates excess energy that can distract you, so we say chew away!

Go ahead and gnaw at the wood of your favorite pencil brand, or bite the cap of every pen at your desk. You can stick your pen in your mouth and pull it side to side; you can chew on a pencil eraser, leaving bite marks along its length. No matter your method of fidgeting by chewing a writing utensil, it's both enjoyable and helpful.

If you've ever felt anxious trying to keep your pens and pencils out of your mouth, you already know a little about how this fidget works. Putting a writing utensil in your mouth, according to researchers, forces you to use the very same muscles that get used when you smile. Every bite and gnaw relieves stress and makes you feel happy—you're almost tricking yourself into enjoying your work. The movement of your facial muscles also means you don't have to sit entirely still while listening, thinking, or reading. This small motion sends those feelings of distraction out of your mind and into your muscles, helping improve your focus while you bite. ■

TASTE SOMETHING SUGARY

Stop avoiding sugary drinks and improve your attention span by sipping on sodas and juices—just try not to drink too much of them in the process!

A surprising sensory fidget, sipping a sugary beverage gets your mind back on track without being distracting or time consuming. The fidget is an easy one to follow: take a sip of lemonade, soda, or juice. Swirl the liquid around in your mouth, then spit it out into another cup or straight into the trash. The trick is to swirl, or taste, drinks made only with real sugar; artificially sweetened drinks made with Splenda don't have the same effect.

Sugary beverages are energy boosters thanks to the excited "high" they create, but because sugar causes attention and focus to plummet when the crash hits, they aren't thought of as beneficial productivity solutions. However, researchers at the University of Georgia have discovered that just a taste of sugar improves both mental focus and self-control. When individuals swirled and spat out sugary drinks, they performed tasks faster and were more motivated to complete challenging problems. The sugar stimulates sensors on the tongue, and those sensors connect to the brain's motivation center. It's like a quick shock that nudges your mind to return its attention to work. ■

SIP CINNAMON-SPIKED COFFEE

Coffee alone is a great taste-centric fidget thanks to its hot temperature and caffeine boost, but adding a bit of cinnamon to your cup provides another way to perk up your mind and get yourself focused. Make your usual mug of coffee in the morning or afternoon and add a small amount of cinnamon. Stir to combine, sip away, and reap the benefits from this unique drink. A dash of cinnamon makes you feel alert and reduces feelings of stress or frustration regarding a task or assignment. You can even skip the coffee altogether if you'd like; cinnamon alone gets your attention back on track and improves your mood.

Cinnamon improves mental processing capabilities, making it the perfect choice when you're struggling to complete a task or understand new information. This spicy addition also kick-starts overall brain function, helping you think more clearly and react more quickly. Lastly, visual and motor skills become sharper when you consume cinnamon coffee, helping you fight off the sluggish feelings that come with a dull task or weighty workload. ■

EXPLORE CITRUS

The taste of citrus is like a bright spark that kicks your attention into gear and gets your thoughts focused on the most important parts of your day. The smell and taste of citrus fruits increase speed, hone attention, and improve performance. A little goes a long way, as a whiff, bite, or small sip of orange, lemon, or lime helps ensure you're both paying attention and avoiding mistakes. Research conducted at Reading University found that drinking orange juice increased individuals' work speed and ability to focus on mental tests. Other studies found that citrus keeps the mind alert, helping maintain steady concentration during tricky tasks and performance consistency for as long as 6 hours.

Fidget your way to better focus with the following citrusy ideas:

- Drink a glass of fresh orange juice
- Sip strong, sour lemonade that mimics the taste of real lemons
- Drop a lemon slice into your water
- Chew on orange slices
- Add a splash of lime to any beverage
- Cut open a citrus fruit and keep it nearby while working, allowing you to inhale its scent ∎

ENJOY GINGER CANDIES

Ginger candy might sound like an unusual choice, but sucking on this slightly spicy, somewhat bitter hard candy does wonders for focus. All you need to do is take your time breaking the candy down in your mouth, savoring and swallowing it to its very end. The actual fidgeting involved in eating the ginger candy helps exert distracting energy, but the crucial element is the ginger it contains. Sucking on ginger improves both memory skills and attention span, keeping information in your brain as you learn and ensuring your thoughts don't wander to an entirely new place.

Make sure that the candy you choose contains real ginger extract or root. It's the plant itself giving you a boost, so artificial ginger flavoring doesn't add anything to this simple fidget. A favorite herbal remedy of many, especially in Asia, ginger helps cognitive function in a number of ways. Furthermore, ginger makes your reaction time faster, aiding you as you try to speed through your workload without losing your motivation or squandering your attention span. Your brain and your productivity will thank you for this unusual and tasty form of fidgeting. ■

SNACK ON YOUR FAVORITE CHOCOLATE

Scientific research has been kind to chocolate in recent years, discovering a wealth of health benefits in many varieties. We now know that chocolate can boost cognitive performance and lengthen the duration of your concentration, improve working memory and organization, and help abstract reasoning, as well as scanning and tracking skills.

Snack on a small piece of dark chocolate while you work and you'll improve your focus, remember facts and details more easily, and stay on top of challenging tasks.

Psychologist Merrill Elias and researcher Georgina Crichton found that choosing chocolate as a snack affects cognitive function in a few different and positive ways. The duo's research compared chocolate eaters to non-chocolate eaters and found that the cognitive capabilities of those who ate chocolate were significantly better. Chocolate fans performed better on small tasks, too, such as recalling series of numbers or lists of information and multitasking. Bite into chocolate, and everything from your shopping list to your screenplay will become easier to focus on. ■

DELAY THE JOY OF CHOCOLATE

Although chocolate brings cognitive enhancement when eaten, choosing not to eat that very same snack can also help you fidget your way through a task for better results. Place a piece of your favorite chocolate within reach, and your focus will strengthen while you avoid the treat in question. Resisting the temptation to enjoy chocolate may seem a "tasteless" way to fidget, but choosing to delay a delicious treat for even a short time improves focus, can lead to better performance on tasks, and helps keep distractions at bay.

Part of the reason distractions are so appealing is their promise of gratification—we want to give in and give up to enjoy something more exciting and more rewarding than a challenging or boring piece of work. In 1968, Walter Mischel began conducting "marshmallow studies" that tested delayed gratification and its impact. Children who resisted taking a marshmallow placed within reach were rewarded with a second treat. Yet the rewards extended beyond another marshmallow. Those who practiced delayed gratification performed better academically and achieved better test scores, coped with stress more effectively, and were better at resisting distractions. The benefits of saying no to chocolate, even just temporarily, translate into better focus and distraction elimination. Put off a piece of mouthwatering chocolate rather than giving in to the urge to snack on it, and success in maintaining focus becomes easier. ■

SUCK ON LOLLIPOPS (OR HARD CANDY)

Keep your tongue, teeth, and taste buds engaged while you plan, prep, clean, organize, or file, and you'll hold your focus on a given job for a longer period of time. Pop a piece of hard candy into your mouth and take your time sucking on it, moving it around as you enjoy its flavor. Any food item that takes a while to eat or break down in your mouth is an excellent source of fidgety fun. The following make for great tasty fidgets:

- Peppermint candies or candy canes
- Sticks of rock candy
- Thick, solid squares of caramel
- Popsicles
- Flavored hard candy discs
- Hard breath mints

The act of sucking on a hard object like a popsicle or lollipop connects to our oral sensory skills. Kids often demonstrate how sucking streamlines attention and regulates the body: children are constantly putting things into their mouths, seeking stimulation and movement as an outlet for their energy and desire to move. Sucking something slowly and turning it over in your mouth, letting it hit your teeth, is soothing and calming while also active. Like chewing and physical body movement, this act "distracts" the extra energy that drives us to want to move around and frees up our brain to focus. Until the candy breaks down, you can move it around and crunch it to pieces to keep your central focus on something more important. ■

EAT SOMETHING SUPER SOUR OR SPICY

The sharp sting of an incredibly sour food and the slow burn that spreads through your mouth from spicy snacks are sensations you can turn into fidgeting methods. Whether you love the zing of spicy and sour treats or cringe with every bite, these two extreme taste profiles can give you a jolt of improved focus along with that incredible shock of flavor. Choose a spicy or sour food that carries a powerful punch of taste—something that doesn't register as very spicy or super sour for your taste buds won't pack enough of a punch.

Try a sour, spicy treat like:

- Dill pickles
- Lemon juice (not sweetened)
- Spicy salsa
- Sour gummy candies
- Fresh jalapenos (or other fiery peppers)

The connection between spicy or sour foods and focus is similar to the phenomenon that happens when you enjoy a hard, slow-to-dissolve candy like a lollipop. A strongly spicy or sour food stimulates receptors inside the mouth, providing a welcome distraction that redirects your focus. The hit of flavor—as well as the burning feeling occurring as you eat—is something new and completely different from what you're trying to concentrate on, helping occupy the distractible part of your mind while you turn your attention to whatever else is before you. ■

DRINK A THICK SMOOTHIE OR MILKSHAKE

There's nothing quite like a thick, cold milkshake: it's refreshing, sweet, and sometimes difficult to drink. The best milkshakes need a little time to melt before they're easy to sip. Before your milkshake liquefies, though, turn it into a tasty fidgeting method. Struggle through an incredibly thick milkshake, or try to suck a chunky smoothie through a skinny straw when your dedication to an assignment or piece of work starts to slip.

According to scientists and sensory learning therapists, trying to consume a difficult food or beverage, like a gooey square of caramel, directly impacts your attention span. The trigeminal nerve, which is located in the face, is what helps us feel the sensations of biting, chewing, sucking, and moving our mouths. That important nerve stretches its branches up into the brain stem, where it works to control the sleep-wake cycle, levels of alertness, and focus or concentration. When the trigeminal nerve is stimulated, it helps wake up the brain and send signals of alertness. So, as you try your hardest to suck that smoothie through a straw, your nerves are signaling that it's time to focus and get some work done! ■

DRINK SOMETHING SUPER HOT (OR COLD)

A steaming cup of coffee or tea in the morning provides a nice, warm wake-up call. That hot beverage also works to get you focused and ready to settle in for a lecture, meeting, or long workday. Ice-cold drinks work in a similar manner: they wake the body up, getting your blood flowing and your brain activated for the day ahead. If you're starting to feel your attention wane, pick up your favorite extreme-temperature drink for another pick-me-up. You can rely on the following to wake up your sleepy, bored brain and stimulate your mind enough to focus once again:

- Hot coffee or tea
- Piping hot chocolate
- Cold (refrigerated or nearly frozen) water
- Extremely cold sparkling water

The goal of this fidget is to choose a drink at one extreme or the other: very hot or very cold. It doesn't actually matter what's in the beverage itself; its extreme temperature is what does the trick. Piping hot and frosty cold drinks both improve focus during reading and listening (such as in meetings) by activating temperature sensors in the skin. These temperature extremes increase the heart rate, provide a surge of adrenaline, and make you feel awake and alive. If you start drifting into dreamland, drink something hot or cold to activate that adrenaline and get yourself pumped up anew. ■

PART 4

SOUND

FIDGETING BY LISTENING

Often dismissed out of hand as a distraction, sound plays a key role in concentration and productivity. The ambient chatter of family life or the low-level sounds heard in all corners of the workplace can feel disruptive and are often blamed for lost focus and increased distraction. According to experts, different background sounds and noise levels do impact our ability to concentrate—and not in quite the ways we may think. While we might be more attuned to the negative effects of sound—especially if you're someone who prefers absolute silence—scientific research studies have also found that there's focus and productivity hidden in sound.

The connection between concentration and sound, of course, starts with music. The late neurologist and author Oliver Sacks was one of the first to study the impact of music on the brain. Sacks's exploration of music as a form of therapy in turn sparked a whole new field of research, and today the neuroscience community acknowledges that auditory stimulation—the use of sound to fidget your way to improved focus—is a powerful tool. A study conducted by researchers at the University of Illinois at Urbana-Champaign found that when assigned to complete tasks while exposed to sound at varying volumes, people became most creative when working in an atmosphere of moderate noise. Low noise, or the sound level of an average office, was uninspiring. Yet as the noise level and number of decibels increased, participants became more creative and more abstract in their thinking—at least until the volume became difficult to handle.

Exposure to noise alone spurs creativity, but music is where we see the strongest gains in attention spans—listening to music, at least in some contexts, is a way to fidget with our ears and delivers significant improvement in concentration, cognitive capability, and creative thought. Music therapists find that the rhythm of any music provides the brain with structure, calming and soothing the mind with familiar sounds and beats as it struggles to stay focused on a single, perhaps tedious job. Working with music on in the background lights up both the left and right sides of the brain, which is understood to unlock higher levels of cognitive performance. Furthermore, listening to music improves memory by enhancing connections between different areas of the brain that are connected to both our attention and the reward hormone dopamine, according to research published in the *Journal of Cognitive Neuroscience*. Whether it's listening to music or tuning in to some other sort of rhythmic noise, fidgeting with sound can have a profound impact on your attention span, creativity, and overall level of cognitive function.

Of course, fidgeting with different types of noises and sounds does so much more than "improve cognitive function." It brightens a bad mood, enhances perception while working, and generates better quality of work no matter what you're working on. And we all love music! While it might seem a bit rude to pop on a pair of headphones in the office or shut out your friends during school study periods, it's worth a few words of explanation to those around you—tuning in to the sounds that best help you focus offers big advantages when you need them most.

LISTEN TO CLASSICAL MUSIC

Classical music is often touted as a virtual cure-all: it's relaxing, satisfyingly instructive for young children, pleasing to the ears, and soothing for sleep. Although classical may not be your favorite music to jam to, it's an excellent way to fidget with your ears without lifting a finger. Turn up a Bach playlist, or find some popular sonatas by Beethoven and Mozart. The notes, rhythms, and sweet sounds of these classical tunes stimulate the brain, improving everything from motor skills to mood and creativity. Classical music also aids concentration and focus, keeping your mind on task whether you're cleaning the house, party planning, or reading a brand-new book.

These positive effects of classical music come from what's called "the Mozart Effect." A number of different scientific studies have tested the theory that classical music is the best type of sound to listen to while working. Surprisingly, each of those studies found that the brain flourishes while listening to classical songs, especially the works of Mozart. Overall, the Mozart Effect reveals that classical music helps expand spatial-temporal reasoning—the ability to think about concepts, plans, and more from a long-term perspective—and aids the mind in discovering unique solutions to logic-based problems. Create a playlist of Mozart's most well-known songs, or pick your own beloved classical jams, and you'll increase your concentration while cultivating better cognitive function as a whole. ■

PLAY AMBIENT TECHNO MUSIC OR INTELLIGENT DANCE MUSIC

Electronic Dance Music (EDM) bumps, pounds, fluctuates, and rushes through its beats, meant to draw bodies onto the floor to pulse, move, and flow. Dance music typically captures an upbeat mood, fast-paced and unrelenting in its buzzing, catchy rhythms. Yet dance music—more specifically, Intelligent Dance Music (IDM)—can also be ambient, down-tempo and calmer. Instead of turning on your favorite EDM songs, switch up your to-do playlist with IDM, and you'll achieve better focus without wanting to get up and actually dance. Turn dance music into a fidget by opting for IDM or ambient music: songs that are more random and experimental in their patterns and composition and that use different sound tools like synthesizers.

IDM was created as an in-between step for dancers and partiers who move to electronic dance music for hours and hours. With all of the upbeat sounds and rhythms of traditional dance music, everyone needed a break—and Intelligent Dance Music was made for taking breaks. Down-tempo yet still positive, chill, and modern, IDM is slower-paced and quieter in its sounds than you might expect. It's similar to ambient music made specifically to relax the mind and let thoughts roam while still inspiring creative thought. As a result, Intelligent Dance Music and ambient music are both excellent genres for easing anxiety and stress, as well as improving focus during cognitive tasks that require deep thought, such as hours of in-depth studying or memorization of new material. ■

WHISTLE WHILE YOU WORK

Have you ever stood up to give a well-rehearsed presentation and started speaking gibberish? Maybe you've bombed during a crucial sporting event or gone completely blank in the middle of an exam. One method of sound fidgeting can fix the problem of crumbling under pressure: whistling while you work. Whistling, or humming if you prefer, can improve work performance, calm an anxious mind, and help you succeed under pressure.

Psychologists at the University of Chicago studied how the brain works when overloaded with too many pieces of information. As we juggle responsibilities and tasks, our brains can have too much to process. That overwhelmed brain then causes choking—paralysis by analysis, according to the researchers. When we feel as though everything must go "right" or perfectly, our brain starts to overanalyze and process more than it should, leading to disaster.

Whistling, however, prevents the parts of the brain that can interfere with performance from taking control under stress. The act of pursing your lips and concentrating on a specific song relieves pressure on your working memory, the area of the brain that focuses on your biggest, most important task, and turns some of its attention to the smaller distraction of whistling. With your excess or nervous mental energy concentrated on your whistling, you can get to work giving that important wedding speech, hitting a crucial golf swing, or acing a standardized test with better overall performance and a clearer mind. ▪

TUNE IN TO THE TICKING OF A CLOCK

Ticking clocks and watches make sounds that are almost imperceptible—until the rest of the room goes quiet. If you catch yourself unable to hear anything except that rhythmic and repetitive tick-tock sound, give in and let your mind follow the beat. Let the ticking sound fill your ears, resound in your head, and guide your own rhythm. Allow the hard and soft beats of the clock hands' movements to push you, to keep your hands folding or cleaning or whatever else they need to do. The body has an internal rhythm of its own, and that rhythm can be altered by other paced and repetitive beats.

Japanese researchers studied the effects of clock ticking on individuals' performance while working. The study asked participants to perform tasks while the sound of a ticking clock played either quickly or slowly. While the fast clock had no impact on the group, the slower rhythm slowed down the participants' working speed. However, this was found to be a positive effect as the slower pace led to smoother, more accurate work. A slower-paced ticking sound lowered pulses, leading to improvement in quality of work and calmer, less-stressed participants. Zone in on the ticking of the noisy clock in your kitchen or the movement of a particularly loud watch in the workplace, and you'll be able to better complete any task. ■

PAY ATTENTION TO YOUR BREATHING

Breathing is automatic and not something most of us pay much attention to. In fact, it may be such a background activity that you catch yourself holding your breath without realizing it during exercise or breathing shallowly and rapidly while trying to race against a looming deadline. When distractions start to tug at your eyes or your thoughts, take a pause and use the sound of your inhales and exhales as a fidget.

Get your breathing and your brain concentrated with one of the following exercises, listening to the sound of your breath during each:

- Alternate breathing through each nostril. Take a breath in through the left side of your nose, holding your finger against your right; exhale through the left side. Take another breath in through the right side of your nose and repeat several times.
- Take deep breaths with audible exhales. Inhale with your nose, taking a breath that fills your chest with air. Open your mouth slightly and push the air out, hearing yourself exhale.
- Try the 4-7-8 breath pattern. Take a breath inward for 4 seconds, then hold that breath silently for 7 seconds. Blow the breath out with your mouth slowly, counting to 8 seconds. Try to make a whooshing sound as you exhale so you can hear the release.

Fidget with your breathing rhythms and you can sharpen your focus again. Listening to the sound of your own breathing as you follow different exercises draws your mind into what's present and pressing: the emails you're trying to read, the online lecture you're trying to follow, the knitting pattern you're trying to master. Concentrating on the sounds of your inhalation and exhalation, the inward and upward intake and the slow blow outward, allows distractions to fade into the background and renews your focus. ■

REPEAT WHAT YOU HEAR ALOUD

Did you lose focus while chatting with your coworker about the numbers you need to complete a project? Can't remember what, exactly, the caterer said during your phone call? It's easy to lose focus and completely miss information when you're zoning out, especially if the information you're hearing is flat. Take a page from a parrot's book of tricks and repeat what you hear out loud to fidget your way back to a focused, alert mind.

Repeating what's said is a way to keep your ears and your mind focused on what you're hearing without missing a beat. Instead of shifting your attention to people walking around in the background or the dull hum of the air conditioner, keep your focus on the conversation at hand by repeating what was just said. This form of fidgeting offers clarification and makes you engage with the activity in front of you. As an added benefit, you'll also become a better listener by adopting the skills of active listening.

It's not as weird as it sounds. Here are a few examples of how you can practice active listening and repeat what you hear without drawing odd glances:

- Repeat numbers or facts for clarification: "So that's one hundred and sixty-two place settings we'll need for Saturday at nine a.m., right?"
- Acknowledge others' mentions of their feelings or concerns: follow up a comment about deadline-related worries with, "I understand being worried we won't be able to meet that deadline."
- Confirm your own role in a larger project: "Yes, I will be responsible for bringing the cake on June twelfth." ■

LISTEN TO YOUR TO-DO LIST

A to-do list is meant to tighten your focus on the most important tasks you need to accomplish over the course of a day, a week, or whatever the given period of time. They're meant to be concise: only the most important items make the list. Yet obviously the act of creating a to-do list doesn't mean you're going to stay laser focused on those listed projects; distraction can still pull us away from our best intentions. Lists are also easily forgotten, sometimes just a few minutes after they've been made.

Instead of writing your tasks down and moving on, turn your to-do list into a vocal and auditory fidget to keep yourself on track. Once you've crafted your list for the day ahead, take a break every few hours to read what's left on the list out loud. You can also rely on your smartphone, tablet, or other smart device to read your to-do list aloud to you.

The auditory action of listening to our to-do lists forges links between our brain and our ears. Research indicates that the auditory-memory link is strong: subjects who read itemized lists out loud are better at recalling those lists than those who simply scan them visually, probably because visual memory isn't as strong as auditory memory. Hearing rather than just seeing your list makes you more likely to remember, and therefore accomplish, everything on it! ■

READ YOUR WORK ALOUD

Distracted reading is useless reading. How many times have you struggled to understand the words on the page, watching them swim in circles as you reread the same batch of lines repeatedly? The next time you crack open a book, work on analyzing a poem, or craft a letter to your extended family, read your writing out loud as you go. Read entire pages, paragraphs, stanzas, or emails out loud, and you'll fidget your way to improved information retention, better concentration, and increased engagement.

When you're reading while distracted, you aren't engaged with the content or the overall message of what you're reading, and you're less likely to remember what, exactly, you just consumed. Long understood as an excellent approach to editing and correcting written works, reading aloud helps draw your attention to aspects of writing you didn't notice when reading with your eyes alone. Hearing phrases, sentences, pauses, and intonation points out problem areas and statements that are unclear.

Reading your work out loud also brings the words into the brain's memory center, helping to improve your concentration, comprehension, memory retention, and engagement with the words on the page. Students who read material out loud are significantly better at recalling facts and details than silent readers are; research also indicates that reading material out loud helps the brain pay particular attention to words and concepts that are new and different. Fidget with the way you read, and you just might hone your learning skills along with your focus. ∎

MIMIC THE SOUNDS OF A BUSY COFFEE SHOP

If you want to focus your mind, work more efficiently, and spark your imagination, head to your local coffee shop: tune in to the dull murmur of others' conversations; the hum of machines and background music; and the sounds of people walking and moving around, and you'll likely see a positive difference in your output. The sounds of a coffee shop are a great auditory fidget, offering background noise at just the right moderate level that encourages most of our minds to do deeper thinking, with better creativity and increased focus.

This fidget doesn't even require you to leave your house or office! If doing so isn't an option, you can mimic a coffee shop environment and surround yourself with the noises of bustling baristas, coffee spurting machines, and chattering customers by downloading an app or playlist featuring these familiar sounds.

Coffee shops feature ambient noise, the kinds of sounds that are lively enough to capture a small part of your attention yet unengaging enough that you can tune out the details. According to ambient noise research published in the *Journal of Consumer Research*, the buzzy background sounds that can be heard in an average café are the perfect mix for creativity. Broader thinking, creativity, and new ideas sprout when we're surrounded by ambient noise—and the results of several experiments show that moderate noise is just distracting enough to provide the perfect balance for focusing on and accomplishing work. The bland, uninteresting noise helps guide your concentration toward that homework assignment, interesting article, or coding project you're trying to complete. ∎

ENJOY SOME SARCASM

No, really.

The clever wisecracks and snarky quips of your coworkers, friends, and even random strangers can spark creativity and insight as you work on a task. Up your sarcasm fluency and you'll start thinking outside the box, finding new solutions to problems, thinking more clearly and abstractly, and becoming more creative—a perfect mix for better focus during a long, dull task.

What makes hearing sarcasm a fun and effective fidget is the creative basis of sarcasm itself. In a 2005 study, researchers found that sarcasm is a unique form of commentary and mental activity. Many people, including a large number of the study's participants, misinterpret sarcasm and find it difficult to understand. However, the study discovered that those who understood and picked up on sarcasm both in person and via email correspondence were better abstract thinkers. A more recent study from 2015 found that those who could identify sarcastic comments performed better on creative tasks. Being able to pick up on verbal irony and the act of understanding its exaggerated nature requires a creative orientation, and that same clarity and innovative thinking is directly applied to other tasks when you're in the proximity of sarcasm.

Both those who doled out sarcastic comments and those who heard them or saw them written out were seen to reap the benefits of this sound-based fidget. Just make sure you use sarcasm sparingly; those around you might not appreciate your approach to concentrating and sparking creativity as much you do! ■

CHOOSE A LOUD, CLICKING KEYBOARD

No matter how slowly, quickly, softly, or powerfully you type on any keyboard, there's an unavoidable clicking sound that comes with the tap of every key. Some, like many computer coders, enjoy the sound of their fingertips tapping away. If you're something of a quiet key-tapping typist, you can create a clicking, tapping soundtrack for your household chores, data entry, or study sessions thanks to apps and online playlists that loop the sound of typing at a loud keyboard for hours on end. You can also upgrade to a louder keyboard—yes, they sell loud keyboards on purpose—if you want to fidget to get your brain in the zone of concentration every time you have something to type.

Tap into the power of a keyboard's clicking sound and use it as a way to fidget toward better focus and renewed concentration. The underlying logic behind loud, clicking keyboards and the sound of fast, aggressive typing is part mindless motion and part slightly distracting noise. The familiar, repetitive motion of hitting each key feeds the mind's desire to settle on something constant and unexciting. With every loud clicking sound, your brain tunes in to the rhythm of your fingers tapping at each key—and the tapping of typing creates a consistent, ambient sound that distracts just enough to allow your mind to concentrate on the larger, more critical task at hand. ∎

LISTEN TO THE SOCIAL SOUNDS OF PLEASANT CONVERSATION

If the pile of papers sitting before you is numbing your ability to focus, or the stacks of wedding invitations that need to be stamped and sealed are beginning to swim before your eyes, fidget your way back to concentration and refreshed energy by listening to the sound of people talking. Sit in an area that features significant traffic, like the office break room, to fill your ears with conversations. When your focus is starting to fade, you can also strike up a conversation with whoever's nearby—a total stranger is best, but a friend or familiar face works too.

Whether you're sleepy or just mentally burned out by a single task, listening to people's conversations provides the jolt of focus and energy that you need to keep going. Getting a small burst of social interaction is reenergizing, helping you feel as though you're taking a break and becoming engaged with the world beyond your desk, your laundry room, or your classroom.

When getting up and chatting isn't always possible, you can fidget with your ears without leaving your seat by listening to realistic conversations on web videos and achieve the same positive effects. Listening to a soundtrack of people talking also provides ambient background noise while you work, letting your brain both tune in and tune out so you can better focus on licking those envelopes or sorting through those papers. ■

ADD THE SOUNDS OF NATURE TO YOUR SPACE

A river running over rocks and splashing against sandy banks; leaves waving in the wind, rubbing against tree branches; the whooshing of wind as it blows through tall grass and the trails of the forest. These nature sounds and many more are auditory fidgets, featuring low-level noise that soothes while providing a small amount of stimulating distraction. Whether you choose to use a playlist, app, or other white-noise device with a nature sounds setting, the noises of trees rustling, animals chattering, and brooks babbling work to improve concentration, soothe feelings of stress, enhance productivity, and boost your mood.

Just as looking at images of nature and greenery—the visual version of this fidget—offers a boost in concentration and a shot of energy, so too does tuning in to a soundtrack of nature's most familiar noises. Research conducted by scientists at Rensselaer Polytechnic Institute studied the incorporation of nature sounds into the workplace and found the benefits were substantial for focus, stress, productivity, and overall mood. Researchers played nature-based sounds, such as flowing water from a stream or the crashing waves of the ocean, while participants worked as they normally would in an office setting. The researchers found that natural sounds helped employees block out more distracting noises, such as a loud meeting or laughter from a break room, yet weren't so loud or unpredictable that they negatively impacted focus. Rather, the background sounds of a breeze blowing, a whale cooing, or the patter of raindrops made individuals happier while working and more focused on their projects. Nature, unlike white noise, causes a relaxation response in the brain that alleviates stress and instills calm. The combination of soothing and minimally distracting nature sounds makes for more effective and productive people, whether you're working on reorganizing your closet or crafting your next presentation. ■

TUNE IN TO THE SOUND OF CHANGING BEATS

Classical music and Intelligent Dance Music bring brain benefits when it comes to fidgeting and focus, but other types of music help concentration too. One example is music with a set number of beats that changes subtly as a song plays. What is it about those specific kinds of songs that lure us into the perfect focus with the sound guiding us to keep our attention on task?

Part of the fidgety magic of music lies in a song's number of beats per minute and how those beats change once you're entranced and focused to keep your concentration steady. When you listen to music, you're giving your brain something to amuse itself with, letting your mind engage with the sounds yet not pull your attention completely away. Songs with 128 beats per minute, with each beat separated by approximately 120 milliseconds, are best, according to music productivity expert Will Henshall. Henshall also recommends music that increases its beats every so often, upping from 128 to 132 beats per minute. This change ensures that your brain remains interested and engaged, which in turn keeps your focus locked on whatever you're working on. You won't even notice the change in beat, but your subconscious will, and the results will show in increased productivity. ∎

PUSH AND POP SUCTION CUPS

There's something so satisfactory about yanking a suction cup off its flat, tightly sealed surface and hearing the loud pop that results. Play with the sound once, twice, or for a full minute when you need a brain break—or keep one hand on something that suctions so you can create the sound repeatedly while trying to think. If the sucking snap sound pleases your ears, use it to fidget your way to stimulated focus that gets you engaged in your work.

While suction cups do have a physical, tactile side as a fidgeting tool, the sound is what carries the greatest impact and positive effect for many. The sound generated when a suction cup is freed is stimulating, capturing the brain via auditory connections. When you find yourself waning in the face of a chore that isn't interesting or thought provoking, you can reengage your brain and restore your attention by creating the familiar and somewhat surprising sound that comes from suction cups.

Some different types of suction toys that make the most perfect pops (and can also fulfill other forms of fidgeting) are suction construction sets, or small colorful suction cups that secure onto one another or on any flat surface, and water timers with a suction base. These exciting suction cup items combine visual fidgets and touch fidgets with satisfying sound that aids concentration, creating a fun and inviting way to focus. ■

LISTEN TO MUSIC MADE BY BIRDS

Take your nature-sounds fidget a step further for improved focus: fill your ears with the sounds and songs of birds. The notes of a nightingale's song, the continuous patter of a woodpecker, the chirps of a blue jay, and a dove's cooing all create the same effect: cognitive stimulation that increases focus, betters brain function, and invigorates energy.

According to several studies, bird songs both relax and stimulate the brain. These songs signal that the sun is rising and the day is beginning; they're familiar sounds that we hear each and every day. At the same time, the clattering of birds marks the cycle of dawn and evening to our internal clocks. So, when you're staring mindlessly at a task you just can't drum up focus for, like a series of boring homework questions or sorting through survey responses, birdsong lifts your energy levels and increases your ability to concentrate.

Whether you choose to listen to a birdsong soundtrack in a normally quiet environment or use the chirps and tweets to drown out more distracting noises, this auditory fidget will improve your attention and ability to knock projects off your to-do list. ■

TAP ALONG WITH YOUR OWN MUSIC

Have you been guilty of moving along with background music, making your own noises with a pen, your fingers, the palms of your hands? Don't stop snapping your fingers or playing your own role as a member of the band from your desk, laptop, or any other surface. Contributing your own noise to different songs is a way to fidget with your ears—one that increases attention span and fires up the brain to process information more efficiently.

According to a Northwestern University study, the key to capitalizing on this auditory form of fidgeting is engagement. In order to gain increased cognitive benefits from any music, you need to become connected to and invested in the sounds, the rhythm, and the patterns. The Northwestern team studied kids sitting in music class and the impact of merely listening to music versus active engagement. Students who participated with the music, even in small ways, exhibited stronger neural processing. Furthermore, students who continued to be active participants when music played improved their reading skills.

The connection between listening and actively joining in with music, such as through tapping your fingers, drumming your own background sound with your pens, or slapping your hand against a surface, rewires the brain. As you listen and make your own noise, the mingled sounds fill your ears and activate those important neural processing skills. Those simple taps, beats, or even snapping sounds are making you more engaged with what you hear as well as what you're trying to concentrate on. ■

PART 5

TOUCH

FEELING AND FIDGETING WITH DIFFERENT TEXTURES

Chances are that at some point in your life you've been instructed to keep your hands to yourself, to just stop touching everything around you. Can't you just keep your hands still? Sometimes, the answer is no. Sitting completely still and trying not to move a muscle is mind numbing and unproductive, especially for those of us predisposed to getting involved in whatever environment we're inhabiting, touching and feeling everything that's new, different, or unfamiliar. The urge to touch a perfectly smooth hardcover book, poke or squeeze a squishy ball, or manipulate a bendy paper clip into new shapes stimulates the senses, and by doing so, improves our attentiveness and ability to focus on input from the world around us.

Though touch receptors are located in a variety of different places throughout the body, the highest concentration of these special physical receptors are found on our fingers. When our fingers encounter a surface or an object, our touch receptors send messages to the brain that help us experience and interpret what exactly we're feeling. They translate the differences between hot and cold, soft and sharp, texture and smoothness. Our fingers also act as a channel from the extremities of our bodies to the centermost areas of our brains. The motion of our hands and fingers helps dictate how interested or involved our mind is. When you're performing an excessively repetitive motion with your fingers—like typing, writing, or digging—stimulation soon fades, focus eventually wanes, and your brain loses interest.

We first explore touch as babies and small children, but it remains a critical and underappreciated sense long after childhood. Many people do their best learning through kinesthetic, or bodily, stimulation, relying on touch to glean new information while walking, exploring textures, painting, and other physical acts. When you feel your hand gravitate toward the teeth of your jacket's zipper, to the smooth surface of a set of worry beads, or to the sticky composition of putty, you're subconsciously seeking something that will provide sensory input to your brain. Touching something that's enjoyable, distracting, or even unusual occupies this part of your brain and calms the nervous system, keeping your mind on track and helping block out sensory details that clamor for (but don't need) your attention.

There are countless ways to fidget using touch, all of them involving the hands in some way—and it's the manipulation, the turning, rubbing, bouncing, flipping, and feeling we do with our hands that activates the brain, according to NYU's Game Innovation Lab. These kinds of movements build connections between our cognition and our senses. Every time you fidget by folding a piece of paper or rubbing the hem of your shirt, you fire up your concentration capabilities.

Feel out your desire to fidget, and you'll filter out all distractions while focusing your energy on whatever's in your hands. The key to capitalizing on the increased productivity, creativity, and brain activity that comes with fidgeting via touch is to make each motion meaningful. Rather than repeatedly touching a rough fabric or clicking a pen open and closed, allow yourself to touch and feel as your body's instinct sees fit. Let your hands explore the world again and you'll unlock greater creativity, new inspiration, and renewed vigor—all of which will lead inevitably to better results with whatever you're trying to tackle.

SQUEEZE A STRESS BALL

Stress balls may be meant to relieve stress, but they're also just fun—fun to move, manipulate, and squeeze. These enjoyable squishy balls are ideal fidget toys because of their amusing and soothing nature. There's benefit in both physically pressing the ball and feeling it reinflate with life after its compression. The results of a study that examined middle school students' attention in classrooms suggested that providing stress balls to the students created more engagement and better focus, as well as a significant improvement on graded assignments. Your ability to pay attention, consume information, and be productive can all increase with a stress ball.

While working on a large task, the act of squeezing a stress ball generates stimulation for both the hands and the brain. As you feel the ball in your hand, changing it from round to flat, from full to squished, you're giving in to a small distraction that keeps your focus on the larger issue or project before you. Kinesthetic learners in particular adore stress balls as a sensory method of fidgeting; they help information processing, keeping the mind attentive to a lesson or influx of knowledge while providing a sensory outlet.

You don't have to use a traditional stress ball to reap these rewards. In fact, you can use anything that can be squished and brought back to life, such as:

- Nerf footballs
- Defrosted gel ice packs
- Clay or putty
- Mouse pads with gel wrist protectors
- Rubber squeeze toys
- Soft erasers that can be kneaded and manipulated

If you can squeeze it tightly in your hand and then allow it to release, anything with a rubbery makeup can become the fidget tool that keeps your mind stimulated in the midst of even the most boring activities. ■

CLICK YOUR PEN LIKE CRAZY

The compulsion we have to grab any pen we can get our hands on and start clicking away is a fidget based in touch and feel, partly attributed to the joy of the up-and-down motion and partly attributed to the feeling of centering your thumb atop the tiny button. You probably have this fidget mastered already: there are as many varieties of pen clicking as there are of pens themselves. According to educators and experts alike, the fidgeting act of clicking pens is ideal for focus. Though it can be a little distracting to others—breaking one of the cardinal rules of choosing a subtle fidget, unfortunately—this fidget helps direct focus by spurring thinking and processing. Most often, when students in a classroom are clicking their pens, they're facing a tricky assignment or test question; the physical feeling of the pen top satisfies restlessness and allows the brain to train its attention on the question at hand. Pen clicks keep the hands busy, retain focus, and provide a small bit of fun that balances out the boring work happening in the classroom. Beneficial beyond the classroom, clicking your pen can channel your focus if you're creating a shopping list, writing instructions, or...whatever! ■

PLAY WITH YOUR HAIR

Have you been called out by friends, family, or complete strangers for excessive hair-play? Go ahead and twirl away—you're stimulating your brain and getting blood flowing to the head (both beneficial ways to achieve better focus). From tucking loose strands back behind your ear to smoothing frizzy sections repeatedly to combing your fingers against your scalp, getting touchy-feely with your locks is a common and effective fidget.

Some believe it to be a sign of nervousness, while others consider it a quirky personal trait. For most of us, touching and moving our hair is a method of trying to regain focus and fight off sleepy, distracting feelings.

When you play with your hair in any fashion, from gentle tugging to sweeping it off your shoulder to wrapping strands around your index finger, you are working out a bit of anxiety and worry. Behavioral specialists and psychologists point out that it is something of a comfort gesture that helps us work through stress, which is why we often touch our hair in tense moments. Yet the act of touching soothes those feelings, and the texture of hair can also smooth out distractions. As you subconsciously touch your locks, you're giving yourself an outlet to fidget and get your brain concentrated on whatever lies before you. Some also argue that moving your hair around invigorates blood flow to the scalp, waking up the mind and reenergizing your attention span.

The only "rule" to remember for this touch-based fidget is to make sure you aren't veering into dangerous territory by unconsciously yanking on your hair! Gentle flipping, smoothing, and moving is enough to make playing with your hair an effective fidget. ■

MAKE YOUR OWN ORIGAMI

If you want to fidget via touch and feel, try your hand at some origami. Origami is a careful art, one that requires neat folds, expert geometry, and an ability to follow instructions. Yet origami, whether exhaustively practiced or thrown together at the spur of the moment, is a great fidget for those who want to exercise their logical thinking, improve their concentration, and better their math skills. You don't need to carry an origami kit with you for whenever the mood strikes; rather, you can rely on any paper nearby and your own creativity to fidget. Grab a piece of paper—one that you won't need later—and start folding. Fold as you please, feeling the texture of the fold lines, the light indents of the creases, the increasing of the paper's thickness. It doesn't matter what you make as long as you feel your way through the process.

According to learning experts at *Edutopia*, origami gives a number of different skills a beneficial boost: thinking, comprehension, problem-solving, concentration, and dexterity. When fidgeting by folding paper, you're constructing your own shapes and designs, spurring creative thinking and new perspectives. You're also developing your own solutions and approaches, opening your mind to seeing from new angles. As you feel your way across lines, sharp edges, and smooth surfaces, your concentration improves. What you touch and encounter with your fingertips will allow the brain to experience new activity, generating new focus that it didn't get from your other, less engaging task. ■

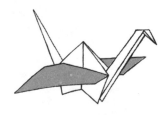

RUB A SMOOTH STONE

A nice smooth surface makes the perfect fidget for those who prefer slick and unblemished textures against their fingertips. Grab a polished rock, a slick disc, or anything that features at least one ultra-flat, smooth side.

A smooth stone, also sometimes referred to as a "worry stone," is a fidget device that you can carry in your pocket, set on top of a table, or hold in your hand. Keep one nearby when you're invested in a task that requires a bit of fidgeting on the side, and you can stroke the stone any time distraction comes to mind. A smooth worry stone, or similar object, allows you to satisfy your unconscious need to touch, feel, and move without losing focus; instead, you'll remain awake, alert, and free of any anxious jitters.

Additionally, when you fidget with something that's perfectly smooth, your hands glide over and against the item with little to no resistance. Your brain doesn't have to think very hard about what it's feeling and encountering; it just enjoys the smooth texture. Repeatedly rub your fingers or palm over the smoothest side of a stone, and you'll create a mini meditative state in your mind. This shifts your attention back to what you're actually trying to focus on: the sentence you lost track of mid-thought, the final item you need for a school project, or the answer to a multiplication problem. ■

MOLD A NEW CREATION OUT OF CLAY

Plop a pile of putty or a clump of clay on your favorite workspace, and you can fidget as often as you like—without making a scene! Some call their lump of clay "thinking putty"—it's a great nickname for a fidget tool that excites the brain, encourages thinking, and draws your attention back to your central activity. Flexible, slightly sticky, and easy to dig your fingers into, clay acts like a stress ball: it provides a sensory outlet to intensify attention on a primary task, and it awakens the brain as it is touched. Every smash of your palm into a mound of clay, each creation you shape, and every dip, divot, and line in the molding material fields distractions through touch and feel.

The slight movements that come with pulling, molding, and smashing clay or putty also do wonders for your focus. According to a 2008 study, allowing students to make slight movements while trying to concentrate on schoolwork led to increased attention, better note taking, more engagement during discussions, and more mental stimulation, all of which made the students better able to consume and retain information. In addition to stress relief and improved attention, touching and feeling the clay itself provides even more mental advantages that can help you master anything, from listening to a long lecture to staying focused during brainstorming sessions. ■

TAKE A RUBIK'S CUBE PUZZLE BREAK

When was the last time you tried to solve your Rubik's Cube? It's been a fixture in homes and offices since the 1980s, but many of us—okay, most of us—have never gotten around to actually cracking this tricky cube. In the years since its release, the Rubik's Cube has become one of the world's best-selling toys. Yet the colorful toy is more than something to play with; it's a smart fidget to keep nearby when tackling any project that requires deep cognitive focus. From sharper problem-solving skills to new perspectives, patience, and improved concentration, spending a few minutes with the Rubik's Cube for a quick break hones intellect and attentiveness, all with just a few twists of a toy.

Turn a distraction into a contemplative, engaging puzzle by grabbing your Rubik's Cube when you want to increase your focus. The puzzle is especially helpful because it's a brain teaser, the ideal type of game to keep your mind sharp. Instead of staring at a blank computer screen waiting for genius to strike or glaring at a pile of party RSVPs that aren't going to sort themselves, try your hand at matching up the colorful rows of a Rubik's Cube. No doubt about it, this brain teaser is incredibly challenging, but it just might help you see your problem, workload, or to-do list in a different way—and when you put the cube away, you'll find yourself refreshed and ready to return all of your attention toward the task you need to complete. ▪

FEEL, FLIP, AND FOCUS ON YOUR KEYS

Toddlers love to fidget with keys, so if you're looking for increased concentration while mastering an assignment or task, follow in their footsteps and grab a set of shiny metal ones. Though this fidget tool does generate what may be unwelcome sound, the jingle of keys isn't the important component of this tactile fidget; it's the different textures present in each key on your key ring. As you hold your jumble of keys in one hand, run your fingers over the different textures. Feel their smooth, unblemished surface; note their grooves and dips; touch the jagged edges of the keys' teeth. Dialing in to these sensory details improves your focus.

When you feel your way around your key ring, you're tapping into your tactile learning and sensory integration needs. Tactile learning helps us experience our environment through touch and feel, and sensory integration is the way in which our brain takes in important information about what it is that we're touching and experiencing. Part of the brain engages with the sensory details of feeling your way through the keys, while the other areas are free to focus on what you're actually supposed to be doing. Grab your keys when you need to think through your next steps at work, or run your hands over them while you're analyzing and editing a piece of writing, and you may find yourself a bit more invested in what you're doing. ■

STICK A VELCRO STRIP ON YOUR WORK SURFACE

Glue a few strips of Velcro to your workspace, and you'll devise a sensory fidget that capitalizes on the textures of sharp and spiky as well as soft and fuzzy. Velcro is the best of both worlds for fidget fans who love to touch while they think. What you feel is important; as you move your fingers and palms over this textured fastening material, pay attention to the loops of fluffy fabric that are soft and soothing, as well as the prickly pangs that arise when you touch the rougher half. Feeling different textures, like the two opposite sides of a strip of Velcro, while trying to concentrate on a job can spark new levels of focus, encourage better performance and productivity, and foster clearer thinking.

First utilized by teachers with antsy, fidgeting students who struggled to pay attention, attaching Velcro to tabletops or the underside of desks satisfies our subconscious desire to move while concentrating. Instead of denying the urge to move, to touch, to learn kinesthetically, give in and allow yourself to feel—it will let you devote more energy to paying attention or focusing on a chore. Quietly feel the soft or more textured side of a Velcro strip while you consider what else you need to add to your email, while you determine what needs to be cleaned out of your closet, or what you need to take notes on. ■

PLAY WITH A SLINKY

You probably played with a Slinky as a child, of course without realizing that you were enjoying one of the earliest mass-produced fidget toys. For years, psychologists and learning specialists have relied on the Slinky to help extra-active individuals train their hyperactivity, making it a fidget tool that's tried and tested. Playing with a Slinky breaks the brain's desire to get up and move while performing dull work, allowing you to play away your extra, distracting energy and dedicate every ounce of focus toward what's most important.

Pass a Slinky between your hands, allowing it to jump on its own while you feel the shift of its weight, or stretch the coil out and run your hands along its bumpy curves. Or, have more traditional fun with the toy and watch it walk down stepped surfaces by itself.

Choosing to intentionally distract yourself with some form of play encourages and allows for freer thinking, increased creativity, and enhanced productivity, making you more efficient and focused when you return to your desk, your laptop, or your household chores. Your sensory toy doesn't have to be a Slinky—it could be anything that helps your hands feel and fidget while you're performing a repetitive, mind-numbing job. You could use a fidget spinner, a bendable bike chain toy, or anything else that combines texture and fun. ■

ADD A TEXTURED GRIP TO PENS AND PENCILS

Pens and pencils are a popular fidget tool because they're almost always close at hand. They're durable enough to bite, clickable, and even bouncy if you play with the eraser end.

Upgrade your writing utensils with special enhancements like grips and toppers, and you can add even more productive fidgeting fun. Add a special grip that's squishable, bumpy, spiky, or moldable, or choose a topper that's decorated with dangles, spinners, or decorations you can rub, move, and feel. Use your adorned writing instruments for any task that requires significant attention: jot down notes, doodle drawings, or make lists and outlines.

Feel your way around your writing tool and you'll achieve a calmer mood, better focus, and the ability to hold your attention for longer periods of time. While your hands consciously or unconsciously move up and down, squeeze and pet, rub and twirl, your mind will remain focused as your fidgeting creates better performance, increased productivity, and makes it easier to turn in good work. ■

POP A SATISFYING SHEET OF BUBBLE WRAP

Whether you're an experienced and practiced fidgeter or someone who's just beginning to explore the fidgety world, popping bubble wrap is a technique with universal appeal. Few things in life are as thrilling as pressing your thumbs into the tiny bubbles and feeling the plastic pop underneath with an audible noise. Popping bubble wrap is certainly a method of relieving stress, with some research suggesting the practice is as calming as a half-hour massage.

According to Western New England College psychology professor Kathleen M. Dillon, who conducted research on the effects of popping bubble wrap, there are two ways this plastic texture-based fidget benefits the brain. First, it keeps the hands busy, the act of feeling each little bubble fueling the desire to get active while at work on a tedious chore. Secondly, the act of popping awakens the individual who's fidgeting. Dillon's study found that participants reported feeling more alert and attentive after popping a series of bubble wrap sheets.

If you'd like a quieter way to feel and fidget with bubble wrap, the manufacturer also makes a version that refuses to pop. Instead, as you push the plastic bubbles, the air merely moves back and forth between different areas, allowing you to reap the benefits without making a single sound. To make bubble wrap ramp up your mind rather than your stress level, seek out this unpoppable stuff! ■

TOUCH THE TEXTURE OF GOLF BALLS

A golf ball is a simple fidget toy with a ton of texture—it's great fun to mess around with. Perfectly round and alternating smoothness with tiny indentations, a golf ball packs a powerful tactile punch. As you play your hands over a golf ball, you don't have to think: the bumpy, up-and-down feeling of the ball helps you fidget into a more alert mind-set without a second thought. When you need something to give your brain a wake-up call or redirect your focus back to an important task, save yourself from suffering through a boring activity by grabbing a golf ball and feeling its every groove.

Touching the bumps and grooves of a golf ball is a sensory fidget that requires just enough attention and interest to re-spark our focus on our primary task. According to authors Sarah D. Wright and Roland Rotz, tactile fidgets that are mildly stimulating and entertaining bring our focus back into whatever dull, uninteresting work sits before us. Feeling your way around, over, and across the dimpled surface of a golf ball also provides sensory change and variation. These two factors perk up both the body and the brain, making you more alert and productive. Incorporate golf balls into these situations to keep your focus and motivation high:

- A long and challenging exam
- A day spent trying to write creatively
- An afternoon of participating in an online course
- A late night of filling out paperwork ■

CLICK, MOVE, AND TOUCH WORRY BEADS

Worry beads don't necessarily mean you have a lot to worry about, but this fidget tool does allow you to soothe your overwhelmed mind so you can achieve better focus, greater productivity, and an improved overall mood. To make the most out of fidgeting with worry beads, try these exercises:

- Line up all of the beads on one end of the string. Move them one by one to the opposite end and repeat.
- Rub the smooth, polished surface of each individual bead, moving the string in a loop around your hands as you move from one bead to the next.
- Twist or bend the string, allowing the beads to hit one another.
- Fold the string in half and grasp multiple beads in one hand. Turn those same beads over in your hands repeatedly.

Worry beads have been a favorite among longtime fidgeting fans—in fact, their origin dates back to ancient Greece, when strands of beads were used both in counting and in prayer. Today, worry beads aren't very different from their original form: a series of beads strung on a looping length of string. Playing with worry beads, whether by feeling their smoothness or moving them back and forth along the string, is calming. Worry bead experts and occupational therapists say this type of fidget toy relaxes a busy mind and helps create a meditative-like state. As you move the beads back and forth or roll and rub them with your fingers, you clear the distractions clouding your concentration, pushing them into the background while returning to your work. ■

ROLL A TENNIS BALL UNDER YOUR PALMS

Grab a tennis ball and put it to work as a fidget device. You don't have to do anything special; just keep the tennis ball nearby and make sure you have a flat surface on which to roll it. When distraction overwhelms your ability to concentrate, use the tennis ball to feel your way back to a focused, productive mind-set. Fidget with your sense of touch, feeling the fuzzy texture, the grooved lines that dip inward, and the printed ink that rises from the surface of the ball.

Roll the tennis ball with one hand, and you can put your other hand to work simultaneously as your brain becomes reengaged with your work. Some educators and psychologists also point to the fact that without movement, the brain grows restless—it wants us to move in different ways, to feel something new that hasn't been repeated over and over for hours. Without that difference or special stimulation, the brain can lose its focus in as little as 20 minutes.

When you put your palm on a tennis ball and roll it around on a flat surface, you create a controlled sensory stimulation that maintains focus, soothes your worries, and even provides the extra benefit of a hand massage. You're also providing an interesting, engaging activity for your brain's sensory center to enjoy—all while your focus grows stronger and you accomplish more. ■

DRINK WATER FROM A SQUEEZABLE BOTTLE

When you need a burst of creativity or a fidgeting diversion to restore your concentration and motivation, take a drink of water. Not any cup of water will do: instead, choose a portable water bottle that requires you to apply pressure into order to take a drink. Lift the bottle as you would normally, squeezing tightly to spurt water out of the top. You don't have to ingest any water if you don't want to. All you need to do is wrap your hand around your filled (or empty) sports bottle and give it a series of squeezes. Squeeze as many times as you like: for a few minutes while you plan the weekend or in quick spurts to jolt your focus back into your work.

Giving a water bottle a good, thorough squeeze works as a quiet, productive way to fidget—it's all about the physicality of squeezing. Feeling the item collapse and reinflate bestows wonderful mental benefits like improved focus and concentration. According to a 2010 study from Israel, this kind of squeezing can induce creativity, and a 2012 German research study found that a good squeeze helps improve performance under pressure. ■

INCORPORATE MOTION INTO TOYS
AND TOOLS YOU TOUCH

Wrapping your hands around any device that produces a light, gentle movement helps clear the brain, provides mental and physical stimulation to dispel away distractions, and facilitates your ability to learn.

According to some grade school teachers and occupational therapists, a subtle, gentle movement that's felt in the hands helps satisfy the fidgeting desire to feel different textures and get up and move around. In fact, without stimulation during repetitive assignments, the brain can start to shut down and attempt to conserve energy. Touch something that's moving just a little bit, and that subtle action will kick the brain's focus centers back online. Try one of the following fidget options to create a slight motion that spurs brain activity, enhances focus, and gets you back to work:

- A half-filled water bottle that allows for sloshing liquid back and forth
- A vibrating pencil grip
- A rubber band that's stretched taut and reverberating with bounces
- A toy that contains an inner ball that rolls or bounces
- A vibrating phone ▪

WEAR A SPIKY OR PRICKLY BRACELET

Carry your fidget with you by wearing a textured bracelet that you can feel while going about your day. Pick a bracelet, or even a ring, that's adorned with sensory and textural details that you can touch and feel whenever distraction starts to creep into your mind. Wearing an accessory that's covered with small points, bumps, indents, or even spikes can make a dramatic statement—yet it also soothes frazzled or stressed-out minds, improves focus, and helps lengthen the attention span. To stimulate your senses and your brain, spin the bracelet around your wrist and let yourself feel every poke and bristle. That small movement will restore focus and aid you in reengaging with reading material, chores at home, or a stack of homework assignments.

Different ways to create a bracelet with spiky, prickly pressure points include:

- Choosing traditional jewelry that features pointed decorative additions or texture on the underside of a bracelet band
- Slipping bobby pins onto a stretchy hair tie
- Adding glue dots to a length of ribbon and wrapping it with the dots side down against your skin
- Wearing a textured stretchable bangle, such as one with raised accents or gemstones, inside out

In addition to wearing something slightly spiky and poke inducing on your wrist, you can also remove it and move the bracelet around in your hands. Turn to your fidget accessory any time you need a touch of concentration or motivation, and the stimulation that occurs with every touch will help to your waning focus. ■

BEND AND FOLD A PAPER CLIP

Paper clips are a favorite fidget toy: they're readily available in just about every workspace, and they're easily manipulated. You can bend, straighten, and feel your away around these flexible metal office supplies—and while doing so, you'll improve your concentration. Make sure that as you fidget with your paper clip you aren't merely moving its wiry body and molding it into new shapes. The benefits come from touch, feeling the smooth metal and running your fingers over the bends and inner spiral. You can also use its thin, relatively flat form and slide it along your fingernails for a different textural impact.

If you don't have a paper clip handy, you can try any bendy metal object, like a bobby pin, a twist tie, or safety pin (though you'll want to be careful and watch out for the sharp end!). As you move the object back and forth, feel its curves, and make new ones of your own by bending and twisting, you'll keep your brain's sensory sections satisfied, freeing up more mental power to direct your primary focus onto your work, whether it's trying to recall your shopping list, diving into a long piece of reading material, or completing an important survey. ▪

INDEX

ABOUT THE AUTHOR

Heather Fishel has written for *WonderHowTo*, *Campus Explorer*, *War History Online*, *Niche*, and *Electronic Retailer Magazine*. She coauthored the 2012 ebook edition of College Prowler's *Denison University: Off the Record* as an homage to the four years she spent writing in the woods of Ohio at her alma mater. When Heather isn't devising new ways to increase productivity with fidgeting tactics or developing entertaining ways to open a wine bottle with a lighter, she's guiding high school and college students through the process of writing their own creative content.